BE AWAKE
AND
PREPARED

A Message from God Given in a Vision

Ernestine N. Moussa

WestBow
PRESS
A DIVISION OF THOMAS NELSON

The Holy Bible, New Revised Standard Version, 2005, Cambridge University Press

La Sainte Bible, Version Semeur, 2000, Societe Biblique Internationale.

WestBow Press books may be ordered through booksellers or by contacting:

WestBow Press
A Division of Thomas Nelson
1663 Liberty Drive
Bloomington, IN 47403
www.westbowpress.com
1-(866) 928-1240

ISBN: 978-1-4497-1809-1 (sc)
ISBN: 978-1-4497-1810-7 (hc)
ISBN: 978-1-4497-1808-4 (e)

Library of Congress Control Number: 2011929844

Printed in the United States of America

WestBow Press rev. date: 6/23/2011

Dedication

I dedicate this book to the lost sons and daughters of the mighty God who still suffer in the misery of this world, forgetting that the Savior has paid the fine and set them free. I hope with all my heart that this book will help them come back to their senses and remind them who they are and what they have in God's house. Whatever they have done, whatever they have become, it doesn't matter. Today, if you hear God's voice, repent and decide to return to his house and you will be welcomed. The loving Father is ready to forget, to forgive, and to celebrate your return. The will of God is to see his children enjoying life abundantly and praise him for his goodness.

Prayer

Dear Father, thank you for your faithfulness. When I was in trouble, you rescued me; you showed me your love and you honored me by calling me your daughter. When I was faithless, you forgave me and renewed your covenant with me. When I was passing through a time of testing, you made it easier by walking by my side day and night. When I was feeling small and weak and unable to reach your most high throne, you came down and gave me your strength. When no one could give me a job, you hired me. Because of your grace, your generosity, and your kindness, I know I will receive all the desires of my heart and you will fill my life with hope, joy, peace, and blessings.

Who am I, that you have chosen me to be your messenger? I am not important, but you have shown your care for me, your servant. I would like to express my love to you with special words and songs that your angels usually use in heaven to express their love for you. Let me sing for you a song of love: "You are the breath I breathe every day. My soul and my heart rejoice in you, my Lord and my Savior. You have been a great God, a great friend, and a great Father to me. I delight myself in your friendship. I praise you for who you are and for all you have done for me and my family."

Please, Father, give the understanding and wisdom to your people and open their eyes for them to see how wonderful you are and to see the place that you have prepared for them for eternity. Thank you for Jesus Christ, who made the sacrifice, died for us, and brought us back close to your throne. In his name, I proclaim your majesty and your power over all the nations of the Earth and over any creature that lives on high in the heavens and down on the Earth. You reign today and forever. Amen.

Contents

Foreword

Finally, here's a book that gives you insight and practical teaching on how to be awake and prepared for the move of God. Ernestine has been given a unique revelation from God that addresses every area of our walk with the Lord. You will be given insight into how to lay foundations for a successful spiritual life.

I believe this book will change your thinking, which in return will change your life. If you are looking for a book that is easy to read but has extensive information to apply, you have found it. Ernestine is truly an ambassador for Christ and in this book reveals how we need his work at Calvary for everyday living.

This book will teach you how to live a life of prayer and holiness. Ernestine goes into detail about how not to be anxious and worried in our daily lives. I am excited about this revelation that has been given to a mighty woman of God for his people.

You will thoroughly love this book and be encouraged as you read it. Are you ready to uncover the new you? Then get ready, find a place to relax, and let God speak to you. Be awake and prepared for change to take place and for the coming of Jesus Christ.

Pastor Chris Aikens
New Life Praise Center
Webb Gin House Road,
Lawrenceville, Georgia

Words of Encouragement

When you feel alone and left behind by society, and when you have been deceived by men, get back to nature. Observe how the grass is green, the trees are dancing with the music of the wind, and the birds are singing and flying in the blue sky. Let this remind you that there is a wonderful God among his creations who did not forget you and who cares about you and is not finished with you yet. You are precious to God than the nature.

Rejoice in the Lord always. I will say it again: Rejoice!
—Philippians 4:4

Acknowledgments

I thank the Spirit of the Lord for this book and for his teachings. Who am I that he has chosen me to be his writer? I give glory to God for everything.

To my pastors, Roger and Chris Aikens: Thank you for preaching the gospel with integrity, honesty, and simplicity of heart. You have prophesied about this book and God has accomplished it. Glory and honor to our God.

I would like to thank with all my heart Pastor Jentezen Franklin for anointing me and for encouraging people all around the world to fast and pray. May God bless you and continue to use you powerfully for his kingdom.

To Pastor Edson Rebustini, my pastor in Sao Paulo, Brazil: God bless you for being a humble, honest, and nice man of God. I thank God for your life.

My beautiful daughters, Gloria and Linda, and my handsome son, Matthew: I love you so much. You bring joy to my life. Thank you for being good kids for me. I am proud of where you are in the Lord. May God bless you and keep you always in his ways.

A special thanks to my husband, Jean Moussa, for humbling himself and letting God's will be fulfilled in my life: I thank God for making you a good husband and a good father. May God keep you safe and bless your life.

To my big family all around the world: brothers, sisters, brothers-in-law, sisters-in-law, nephews, and nieces: Thank you so much for your financial, emotional, and spiritual supports. May God bless you and protect your lives.

The television ministries TBN, DYSTR, ANGEL, 7OO CLUB and many others: Thank you for being a source of inspiration and spiritual education for God's people and for the lost. We learn and receive words of knowledge, revelation, and inspiration from men and women of God whom he is using through your ministries. May God continue to use you powerfully for his glory

I thank with all my heart all my prayer partners and friends for being a solid spiritual support in my life. May God continue to use you and bless your lives.

Introduction

This book is a teaching book with messages from God. The main message of this book was given in a vision. God has always revealed his will to his people in many ways. For this book, God gave me a message through a vision. In this vision, God revealed a secret place where people have to run while waiting for the coming of the Messiah. That place is the only secure place where people will be protected against the horrible events of the last days.

The hand of the mighty God will surround and protect those who have reached that place. In that place, people will find happiness, rest, joy, and peace. God wants everyone to be awake and prepared and to run to that wonderful place and experience heavenly treatment while they are on Earth. This book is based on biblical truth. We will use the scriptures as references to reinforce God's message because the scriptures bring light and understanding. There is no truth outside of God's words.

Every person on Earth would like to live a wonderful life, but many don't know how. Today, people desire to live a good life and will do whatever it takes to have it and to get to what they believe is a place of happiness and peace. People talk about promotion, success, money, and a better life. But by pursuing their dreams, many people leave behind important things such as love, peace, and a relationship with God, family, and friends. They have taken the wrong way to reach the good place.

This world has taught people evil, selfish ways to reach happiness. We can't sow a bad seed and expect to reap good fruit. Bad seeds will always produce bad fruits. It is like going somewhere and taking a wrong turn and expecting to get to your destination. If you figure out early that you are going the wrong direction, you can take a U-turn and go back in the right direction and then expect to get to your destination. But because of that mistake, you wasted time and energy that you can never catch again. It's gone.

Today we are living in a world full of crises, disappointments, and lamentations. The entire world system looks vulnerable and unable to offer stable solutions. I am an economist, and an economist's job is to prevent economic crisis and offer economic solutions. These economic crises are proof that economists have failed and men's sciences are not perfect.

Life is a cycle full of good and bad times. Good times make people happy, but tough times are painful and include a lesson to learn. Usually, we wish only for good things, but bad times happen to good and bad people. The way bad people and good people handle tough times are different. For bad people, tough times are opportunities to complain and to murmur, but for good people bad times are opportunities to learn, to grow, and to glorify the name of God who is able to solve the impossible.

There is a message behind every tough event. Sometimes that event is an opportunity for God to help us redefine our life priorities or redirect people's lives in the right direction and bring them closer to him. Whatever the message behind a tough time is, it serves to push people in the right direction. If people could always discover those hidden messages, understand them, learn from them, improve, and grow, this world could be different.

Where do people have to turn when they are lost and want to learn good ways of reaching happiness? First, we have to believe in goodness and know that we can't reach happiness using evil ways. There is the author of goodness and happiness. His name is Yahweh, God, the creator of heaven and Earth. He has instructions for the right direction to get to that place of blessing. People have to turn to him for help and for wisdom and knowledge.

God, who created the sky, the Earth, and the oceans, exists and lives among his creatures. He has the power to protect, to prevent, and to solve any crisis. He has the instruction book that we need to learn and follow, so that we avoid wasting our precious time. If people seek God in all they do, he will show them what path to take to achieve success, promotion, and a good life. God is almighty. He has the perfection, the control, the balance, the authority, and everything we need.

We are living under God's control and power. God's love is available to both good and bad people, giving everyone the same opportunity. If people continue to ignore God's presence and warnings and don't discontinue their evil ways, they may experience temporary success, but they will never find real peace, joy, or the perfect balance. At the end of time, they will be destroying. We can't live without God's word and expect to succeed. It is written in the book of Psalm, "Understand this, you who forget God or I will tear you apart, and there will be no rescue because you are not grateful and have forgotten that I protect you. I give you the strength to work and the breath to live every day."[1]

These crises are the result of men's imperfections and pride. If we get the message behind these crises and understand that we have been on the wrong path for a long time and make a U-turn, asking God for help, he will take care of our mess and turn it into a blessing. God is able to fix everything. It's never too late to choose God's side. Jesus said in the gospel of Matthew, "But seek first the kingdom of God, and His righteousness, and these things will be provided for you."[2] If we let God take control and lead our life, we will live in the house we didn't build, we will have promotion we didn't work for, and we will experience a good life full of joy, happiness, and peace forever.

A good life is not about getting things, promotions, or money. A good life is when people enjoy what they have and reach the peaceful place where everything is in perfect balance. A good life is all about fulfillment and accomplishment. A good life means life full of peace, joy, and perfect harmony. A good life is about love, relationship, friendship, balance, harmony, fulfillment, and accomplishment. Only God can make life perfect and enjoyable, because he is the author of goodness. If people live far from God's presence, it is impossible for them to reach balance and happiness. People have to decide to make peace with God, with themselves, and with others to experience success, happiness, and joy.

In heaven, the angels, the elders, and all the saints have a faithful relationship with the mighty God. They focus on God's throne of glory day and night. They praise and enjoy his presence. They are not worrying about anything because God provides everything for them. In contrast, on

1   Psalm 50:22
2   Matthew 6:33

Earth, the glory of the kingdom of God has been left behind and people have forgotten that God lives inside them, with them, and has given them everything from the beginning of creation. People are not thankful enough and are not praising him for what he has done for them. They are pursuing perishable things and forgetting about eternal life. They are blinded by material things and don't remember who they are, and they are not worried about where they will be at the end of time.

People have turned their hearts away from God. It is written in the book of the prophet Jeremiah, "Cursed are those who put their trust in mere humans, who rely on human strength and turn their hearts away from the Lord. They are like stunted shrubs in the desert, with no hope for the future. They will live in the barren wilderness in an uninhabited salty land."[3] But if people copy heavenly creatures by focusing on God's throne, thanking God for who he is, and praising him for being among his people, blessings will flow on the Earth and forever they will live the eternal life with God.

This book has a mission of awakening people, refreshing their memories, opening their spiritual eyes, and reminding them who they are and what God has done for them. People will learn why and how to be prepared for God's move in these last days. It will remind them how valuable they are in God's eyes. God keeps sending messengers with his advice to guide people to right paths, but many are still blind and ignoring them.

The vision that God showed me revealed what is going on in the invisible, spiritual world to wake up the minds of his people. By following God's words some people have reached his place of peace, and they are living on Earth like heavenly creatures. Other people are still blind and confused and lost in Earth-limited desires. This vision encourages people to trust God and to move in the right direction. It is an alert to God's people to get ready and prepared for the end of this world.

This is the time of focus and of searching for God's wisdom. It's time to pay attention to what God is saying and follow his instructions. The purpose of this book is to remind people that God wants everyone to be safe and to have eternal life. There is nothing that God cannot do or cannot give to his children. We just have to trust God and make a right decision to follow his way to goodness and reach his place of peace and happiness.

---

3   Jeremiah 17:5–6

This book is an inspiration from the Holy Spirit of God, and it is for everyone who is thirsty for truth, peace, and happiness. We have to take this opportunity to think and to redefine our priorities and decide to live for God only. This book will help those who have never heard the word of God understand and learn about God and his plan of salvation. This book will encourage and push those who are new in the Lord to the high level of knowing him. It will help them stay firm and strong in their walk with God. Finally, this book will help those who know God and have walked with him for a long time to renew their vow of commitment to his service.

PART ONE:

THE ROOTS OF GOOD AND EVIL

Chapter I:

The Vision Given by God and My Testimony

Then, after doing all those things, I will pour out my Spirit upon all people. Your sons and daughters will prophesy. Your old men will dream dreams, and your young men will see visions.

——Joel 2:28

One day I was meditating on the word of God when the Lord suddenly showed me this vision. I saw people up in the sky with peaceful faces, looking rich and very happy. They were wearing some kind of clothes that were white like snow. They were from different nations, of different colors, and both male and female. They all had the same expression on their faces: calm, happy, and peaceful. Each one of them had their hands on something that looked like a jump rope that they were throwing down to the Earth.

My eyes followed the jump ropes to where they were being thrown. From the sky they were letting those jump ropes reach people on Earth. Then I saw on the Earth people who were busy doing their own stuff and not paying attention to those jump ropes falling from on high. The people in the sky were talking, but no one could hear them. A few people saw the jump ropes and were curious to know where they were coming from. Then they approached the jump ropes, and when they were close, they heard the voices of the people on high and saw their faces. They were calling and encouraging them to touch and hold on to the jump ropes and climb up to reach where the people in the sky were living. The ones on high urged and begged the people below to take the jump ropes and reach the sky.

The ones on high explained to the people below why they should decide to join them and how life was better up in the sky. They were happy to share their testimonies with those who were listening to them. By looking at their appearance, you would be convinced. They were looking rich, peaceful, and very happy.

All of them were giving testimony of their past—who they were before reaching the sky and how one day they took the jump ropes, trusting those on high, and reached that place of happiness, joy, and peace. Their lives had been transformed in that place. Many of those who were listening to them were excited to join them and said, "That is all I want, too." They picked up the jump ropes and the people in the sky helped draw them up and continued to encourage them not to give up.

Suddenly when someone was on the way to the sky, some scary and ugly creatures appeared, screaming loudly and breathing fire out of their mouths as if in an attempt to kill those who were trying to reach the sky. It seemed that no one could pass by those creatures because they were acting evil and really ugly. They were very scary looking and were everywhere in the air. It was horrible and scary to see their ugly faces. I closed my eyes because I was scared. But the Spirit of the Lord told me, "Open your eyes and keep looking without fear because those creatures don't have the power to touch anybody who is holding on to that jump rope. Those ugly spirits are only trying to scare and intimidate people and stop people from reaching the sky. Only courageous people can pass by them."

So I opened my eyes and continued to look. When the people who were going up saw those creatures and heard their voices, most of them panicked. Some people let go of the jump ropes, fell, and died; others held on but quickly returned to Earth. But the people in the sky who were pulling them up continued to encourage them not to return to Earth by saying loudly, "Just hold on to our jump rope, hang on, close your eyes. Pay attention to our voices only. Keep coming up, and do not be afraid. Those creatures do not have the power to touch you, and their fire can't burn you because you are holding our jump ropes. Trust us, we passed through there before and we reached this place. Hold on to the jump ropes and focus on our voices and keep coming up. We can continue to pull you up. You are not alone. Do not be afraid, but keep coming up. Do not give up; there is not another way to get here."

Just a few people had the courage to continue going up. I saw them closing their eyes and focusing on the encouraging words of those who were pulling them up, and they reached the sky. The scary creatures did not touch them or burn the jump rope with their fire. The strength and safety of people was in the jump ropes. No one who was holding on was attacked. When those courageous people reached the sky, I saw their faces instantly transformed. They became peaceful and happy, and their clothes were white like those who were there before. In the sky, everybody was dancing and shouting victorious songs. I jumped for joy, too. But only a few people reached the sky.

Those ugly creatures were just there to try to keep people from reaching the sky, using intimidation and playing with their feelings by screaming loudly and sending fire into the air.

Their mission was to terrorize and scare those who were trying to reach the sky, to make them fragile and weak, and to push them to let go of the jump rope and then kill them. Everyone who touched that jump rope was treated like the enemy. The people who didn't close their eyes, and who focused on the creatures' appearance and fire lost control.

Some detached themselves from the jump ropes and died and disappeared in the air. Others begged the people in the sky to let them return to Earth because they weren't yet ready to pass by those ugly creatures. I saw the people who returned to Earth become miserable, losing their joy because they had touched the jump ropes. Having heard the good news of hope, they were seeing happy and peaceful people, but they did not have the courage to pursue their way to the sky. They were resigned and unhappy.

In the sky, the happy people continued to throw their jump ropes to the Earth, but most of the people weren't paying attention; they were too busy and occupied with their own business: buying, selling, planting, eating, drinking, marrying, and having fun, missing the opportunity to save their lives and escape the control of the ugly creatures. It seemed like the Earth was controlled by those ugly creatures. They were attacking only those who listened to people in the sky and had decided to touch the jump ropes and jump up. For the people on the Earth, those ugly creatures were invisible and didn't seem like they controlled them.

After seeing that vision, I felt very sad for those people who died in the air just because they were scared and didn't trust those who called them to help them reach the high place. They were going in the right direction, but they weren't courageous enough to continue and finish their course. It was sad also to see how those who returned to the Earth were miserable. Those people heard the voice of God and had the opportunity to escape the misery of the Earth, but somehow they didn't have enough faith and persistence to reach the sky and give up.

I had many questions in my mind. What did this vision mean? Who were those people in the sky? And why they were throwing those jump ropes to Earth? What did the jump ropes mean? What kind of jump rope couldn't be burned by fire? Where did those scary creatures come from? Why were the people who touched the jump ropes attacked? And why were those creatures trying to keep them from reaching the sky? Why did so many people on Earth not see those jump ropes falling from the sky? I didn't have answers for those questions and asked the Spirit of the Lord to help me and give me the understanding of this vision.

Then the Spirit of Lord said to me, "I know you don't understand, but write this vision. It contains a powerful message from God to his people. It is also a message for those miserable people you saw returning to Earth and for those who are not paying attention to those jump ropes falling from heaven to reach them on Earth. You have a mission to deliver that message, but before that happens, you have to learn many things from God. Stay in God's will and be prepared." After that day, it seemed like the Holy Spirit disappeared from my life and stopped talking and went silent. I remember sharing that vision with my prayer partners, hoping that they could give me some answers, but none of them understood the vision. So I gave up questioning people and continued with my daily life.

My life was busy. I was working for a retail company, going to church, leading prayer at my house with friends, and taking care of my family, being mother and wife as usual. But one year later, things around me began to change dramatically. First, I lost my job; I was fired. The day before that happened I arrived home from work and found my house in a huge mess. I got mad at my husband for leaving the kids unsupervised and letting them made such a huge mess in the house. In anger, I told him I didn't know why I was still married to him. I was mad and said many bad things to him and didn't even care about hurting his feelings. I cleaned the house anyway and went to sleep without apologizing to him.

When I woke up the next morning, all my anger had gone and I was feeling great and ready to go to work. Then my husband woke up, too, and looked at me with an evil eye, something I had never seen before. I didn't understand what was happening to him. Suddenly he began yelling at me in an evil voice, reminding me of what I had said to him the night before and how those words had hurt him badly. Then based on what I had done, he made a list of do's and don'ts that I had to follow; if I didn't, he would leave me and move out.

I was surprised, because the man who was talking sounded like a stranger to me. That wasn't my husband's voice, and his face was scary. He seemed like he was ready to attack me. The expression on his face and his sound of his voice were things I had never experienced before. That man was ready to hurt me, and I decided to run from him as quickly as I could. I went to work. I remember saying to him that it was impossible for me to follow his do's and don'ts list and that if he wanted to move out, he could leave before I came back from work.

It was the first time in eighteen years of marriage that I was afraid of my husband. He had always been a nice man to me, and we never used words like "I will leave you" or "I expect you to leave." That day, I felt that I might choke. I was surprised and hurt badly in my heart. All the words he had said to me and the image of that scary face remained in my mind. That hurt my heart like someone cutting me with a knife a little bit every second. Everything I tried to do that day at work went wrong. I couldn't focus on anything.

During my work hours, I was crying and fled to my car without the permission of my supervisor. The pain in my heart was so strong that I couldn't control my emotions, and I did not want to share my pain with anybody at work. Meanwhile, my supervisor was looking for me. She couldn't find me anywhere and reported me missing to the manager. When I felt a little better, I went back to my position. Then my supervisor asked me where I had been because they had been looking for me and couldn't find me anywhere. She told me that I had to go to the manager's office.

When the manager saw me, he said, "You are fired." I was surprised. How could he fire me like that? I asked him, "Can you give me a second chance? You don't know what is happening in my life right now, and this is the first time that I have done this. I need a second chance." But he said to me, "You were supposed to be in the store because you are on the clock, and you left your position without the permission of your supervisor. You know the policies, and you violated them. I can't tolerate that. This is your end with us. Good luck." He signed my paper and I was fired that day.

I left but couldn't understand why all that was happening to me in the same day. I couldn't stop blaming my husband for everything. I was really mad at him and wished he would leave me alone. I didn't want to see him anymore. It seemed to me that he was responsible for my disgrace that day. When he came home from work, I asked him to take his stuff and leave the house. He looked at me and said, "To go where?" I said to him, "Stop playing with my feelings and my life. I lost my job because of what you did to me this morning. You took revenge and hurt my heart and my feelings. Now you act like nothing happened. If you loved and cared about me; you would have waited for a good time to talk about what I did to you. You have made this day a horrible day in my life. I lost my job and I lost you, too. Now it is too late. I don't want to discuss anything with you anymore. I am really mad at you. I just want you to get out of my life and leave me alone."

He noticed that I was seriously hurt and that I had decided to end our relationship. He said, "What is happening here? Why we are talking like non-Christians?" And he said, "You should see your face and hear your voice. That isn't my wife's voice and your face looks scary. If you are not careful, you will make a huge mistake. Can we just pray and ask God for forgiveness and everything will be okay?" First I didn't like the idea of praying, and then I came back to my senses and realized that he was seeing in me the same thing I had seen in him early that morning. I remembered his evil voice and his scary face, and I hated to hear from him that I looked and sounded like that. I came to the conclusion that something was wrong with us and we needed to pray and forgive each other and pay attention to our feelings and get control over them.

What was happening to us that day was horrible. We came to the conclusion that our relationship was under attack and we needed to fight back. Then we decided to fast and to pray, and we forgave each other.

I began searching for another job, but everywhere I applied they asked why I had left my previous job. The way I was fired was a big issue in finding a new job. When they called my ex-employer, they always found out why I was fired. To make thing worse, a short time later, my husband's small business began to experience losses. He tried to push through by taking a loan from the bank and making the business survive but was not successful. After trying everything to maintain the business, my husband decided it was better to close it.

Now both of us were unemployed and without any income. It was painful. But our faith in God and the joy of our kids kept us strong and alive. We had hope that somehow God would do something and it would be all right. The word of God was our comfort and helped us survive. We learned to keep our faith in God's promises. We trusted him and were sure that he would show up and open new doors.

My husband began his search for work, too, which was hard for him after being self-employed for such a long time. I encouraged him to go ahead and keep trying like I was doing. We had to survive and had the responsibility to take care of ourselves, our three children, and our family members back home. For them and for us, we decided to stay strong, unite our forces, encourage each other, and face the difficulties with faith, patience, honesty, and integrity.

A few months later, my husband found a job, but it was many miles from where we live. He didn't have a choice, and he took it. I remember how the children and I sang hallelujah and thanked God for his faithfulness. The new income was insufficient to meet all our needs, but it was something. We had to eliminate some expenses such as cable and eating out, and tried to survive on what was coming in. The hardest part was when we had to explain to our little children—ten, eight, and six years old—why they couldn't have the same stuff they had had before and why they could not have all they wanted.

Seeing their sad faces was difficult for us, but much more so for my husband than for me. He didn't like saying no to them and kept promising them everything. But the children realized he was lying to them. Then I had to explain to them that Daddy did not have enough money right now and I was unemployed, so we had to have patience and keep praying. I told them we needed to ask our heavenly Father to open new doors for us and said he would certainly listen to our prayers and give us everything we needed and wanted one day.

At that point, we could not use or make payments on our credit cards anymore. Our credit history was messed up. We asked for help from the financial institutions, but with our low income they couldn't do anything. They usually help those who can afford to pay the minimum payment. They convinced us that without another income coming in, filing for bankruptcy was the only alternative we had to get out of trouble. But we didn't want to go that way, so we continued, without success, to look for another job to increase our income. Everywhere there were signs: "Not hiring at this time" or "No applications taken at this time."

Meanwhile, the credit card companies began to call. They were calling all the time. The pressure on us was unbearable. We were treated like thieves. My husband couldn't take it anymore. He began to show signs of depression by complaining about everything. We were crying to God and praying, but it seemed like he wasn't listening. We tried everything to have more income, such as selling things, but nothing was working. Every step we were taking to go forward was somehow failing. After trying to find money to pay our debt without success, we decided to hire a lawyer and finally filed for bankruptcy. It was painful and shameful, but we didn't have a choice.

It seemed like that season couldn't end. On top of all that, my husband became really sick and depressed. He couldn't sleep at night and experienced heart palpitations. He lost enthusiasm and weight, and looked very unhealthy.

One day, he came to me and said, "Honey, you know I love you and I love the kids, but I don't feel strong enough to sustain you with this job I have now. I cannot drive for a long time every day anymore. I drive for long hours and bring less money home. Sometimes I have found myself sleeping while I am driving. It's not good at all, so I have decided to quit this job. I don't know how we are going to survive, but I don't want to die in a car accident." That was the last thing I expected to hear from him.

We had decided to fight this together, but now he wanted to quit his job and quit on his life, too.

My husband was depressed; no longer strong enough to handle the depression we were in. He was weak and seemed like he was giving up on hope. I found myself alone with no one to share my pain, because my partner was weak and sick. And God, on the other side, seemed like he didn't want to talk to me anymore, He was silent and distant. I couldn't understand why I couldn't feel God's presence anymore and why he didn't want to answer my prayers.

I felt desperate and alone and couldn't take it anymore. It was unfair. Seeing my husband down and depressed was the breaking point for me. I couldn't bear it. It was so painful. I realized that the situation was more serious and beyond my control. I could not handle it by myself and decided to cry for outside help. But I knew in the bottom of my heart that God was in control. Even if he was silent and distant, soon or later, he would show up.

So I decided to stay strong and faithful and continue to believe that it would be all right somehow, someday. My husband went to our church and talked to our pastor. Our pastor prayed for him and counseled him to trust God and not give up on him and to keep his job until he found a new one. I explained our situation to my prayer partners and close friends. They prayed for us and everybody asked my husband to not quit his job, to fight for healing and for his family. God would help him, they said, and nothing would happen to him. But my husband kept saying to me, "Why don't any of you understand that I am suffering and could lose my life if I keep driving and working in this condition? I can't take it anymore. I don't like that job, and I can't drive that long every day anymore. I have to quit that job."

Day after day my husband became more depressed. I watched him lose his enthusiasm, joy, and strength to live. I did not understand why it was so hard for him to do whatever it took to keep his family on track until he found another job. I knew he did not like his job or driving so long to get to work, but I hoped he would understand that he needed to do that because he was a father and responsible for his family. That job didn't define who he was; it was just part of a transitional period of surviving.

Sometimes we don't have what we want in life and have to do whatever we can to survive.

Unfortunately, my husband didn't take it that way. He had definitely identified himself as a loser for working for someone else after having his own business, and that made his life miserable and difficult. One day, I observed him from far away, noticing how he took too much time just to stand up from the sofa and more time to put his uniform on to go to work. He was looking very weak and unhealthy, and was suffering from the idea of going to work every day. I had never see him like that before. He was young and full of life, but that day he looked like a very old man. Anyway, I saw him leave and go to work.

After he left, I heard a voice saying to me, "Call him and ask him to quit that job and come back home."

"What? No way," I answered the voice. "How we will survive without any income?"

And the voice said again, "Call him and tell him that it's okay if he quits that job."

It was difficult for me to obey because I couldn't see how we could make it without any income at all. But I took the phone and called him and said, "Honey, come back home. Quit that job. I don't know how we are going to survive, but I want you alive." I explained to him how our kids needed him, how I needed him, and how his family needed him alive, with money or without it. I couldn't continue to see him like that anymore. If he thought that working that job was killing him, he'd better quit and regain control of his life.

Basically I encouraged him to do what he thought was right for him and said that together we would trust God for tomorrow once again. God was faithful; he would provide and would take care of us. So I helped my husband make the decision to quit. I didn't understand why I had to help him quit, knowing we didn't have any other source of income. I was just saying to him what the voice was asking me to tell him. It was like someone telling me what to say and I was just repeating it. It was scary and crazy, but I knew it was God's voice, and I decided to obey and trust it.

After talking to my husband on the phone, something special happened to me. Suddenly I realized that God was talking to me again, and that feeling was wonderful. I wasn't alone anymore. It was like finding an old friend after a long time of separation. From that moment, I was sure it would be okay, because I could feel the presence of God once again and his voice was talking to me again. I was free from anxiety and fear. I gained confidence, and I was sure I had done the right thing by obeying God's voice.

From that moment on, I gave all burdens back to God. I felt like he came to give me a break and to take all my heaviness upon his shoulders. I didn't have to make any decisions anymore. My job was to rest in him and waits to see what God would do. Surely he had a good plan for our life. I decided to trust him and obey him, and peace came back to my heart.

Our friends and family thought it was crazy for a father to quit his job knowing that he was responsible for taking care of his family. They didn't understand why I encouraged him to quit. They were calling my husband irresponsible, but I decided to stay by his side, to help him find peace, restoration, and healing. We had been married for eighteen years at that time, and once again, we decided to stay together, to fight against our fears and frustrations, despite what people were saying about us.

Through all those circumstances and crises, God was teaching me many things. I learned that God can give and can take back. I learned that it is not by our strength that we wake up every day but by his strength. I have seen my strong husband become weak and realized that my husband wasn't my source of provision but that God was. God brings people into our lives as instruments in his hand to bless us. People, jobs, and money can come and go, but God lives forever.

People focus more on things and forget about God, until one day those things disappear and no one is there to help. Then they remember God and cry for help. Only God is a present help in time of trouble. I learned to not take God's blessing for granted and to depend on him for everything every day. I learned also that when God is in charge, every circumstance has to bow down to his command.

When I realized that the presence of God was there with me, I felt in my heart a strong desire to go on a retreat and be alone with the Lord. I had missed him so much and had many things that I needed to talk about and ask. I needed his answers, his instructions, and a clear understanding of what was happening to me and my family. I told my husband I wanted to go on a retreat and be alone with God. We read together in the book of the prophet Jeremiah where it is written, "Lord, you are my strength and my fortress, my refuge in the day of trouble!"[4] Yes, it was a time of trouble, and we needed him to be our strength, our refuge, and our help. We needed him badly.

I left my house, my husband, and my children and went to stay at the house of some friends. They gave me a room for free. I stayed there three days, praying and fasting. On the first day, I could already feel the presence of God in that room. His peace and joy welcomed me there. It was wonderful to be alone with God and forget about the outside world. I felt once again the peace of the Lord in my heart. For almost a year I had been deeply focused on the circumstances around me and my family and had forgotten how good it was to be at peace in the presence of the Lord.

I decided to spend those three days focusing only on God and on every good thing he had done. I began to cry to God and asked him to come and share that time with me. Then I heard his voice saying, "I have chosen you and I will not throw you away. Don't be afraid, for I am with you. Don't be discouraged, for I am your God. I will strengthen you and help you. I will hold you up with my victorious right hand. I, the Lord your God, am here to help you. I am the Lord, your Redeemer."

Yes, the Lord accepted my invitation and was there with me. He never left me, even through tough times. It had seemed to me like I was alone, but he had always been there. The purpose of that pain in my life was to push me toward my destiny. The voice of God kept telling me how through this time of testing he was sharpening me, reaching me from inside and taking out all those things that were consuming me.

God was working in me, making me ready to serve him for his glory. He said, "I am a jealous God and I don't share my glory with anybody or anything. I want you to learn that I am your only source. Only I have the power to give, to save, to deliver, and to provide. And don't worry about your husband and your family; they will be fine, I promise. Now trust me and keep your focus on my job. I will guide your path in the right direction."

On that first day I could feel change in my heart, my soul, and my spirit and everything around me looked different and shining. God's presence filled my heart with his love, his peace, and his joy. I began to

---

4   Jeremiah 16:19

sing and to praise, and I forgot all about the pain, the suffering, the past. It was wonderful. I could feel the hand of God upon me with an exceptional kind of love, making me comfortable and happy.

Then the Lord began to speak to me again and said, "You did good to come before me. Do not worry anymore; everything will be fine. You have passed this test. You have to know that I am your Lord and I love you. You have to come to me for everything. Don't keep your eye and your focus on the blessing but on me, the provider. Your husband and your kids are your blessing from me. I gave them to you not to make your life painful but joyful. You focused too much on them and forgot about me. From now on learn this: your husband is not your provider, and no one can be your provider. I am the source of everything and I am your provider. Know this today: I am the owner of everything, and I am the boss of every boss. When you focus on me, you will never be disappointed. I am the one who protects you, who provides for your family, and who brought you to this country. Never forget that."

The next day the Lord came to me again and asked me a question: "Daughter, what did you do with the vision I showed to you a year ago?"

I answered, "I wrote it down but I never understood what it was about."

The Lord showed it to me again and said, "This vision is a message for my people all around the world. They have to be awake and prepared for the departure. You can't keep it to yourself anymore. Now is the time to let my people know that I have sent messengers among them to help them run to the safe place. The time is now. Go and tell them what you saw in this vision."

Then I asked, "How I will do that?"

He said, "You will write it as a book. This is my message to my lovely people; it is time for them to be confident and take refuge under my wings."

I said to him, "I never wrote a book before. Why me? Who will believe that you have spoken to me?"

He said, "You born for this, Ernestine. Don't worry. I will be with you; I will help and guide you."

"In what language will I write your message?" I asked.

"It will be translated into all the languages of the Earth. But write it first in English."

"But Lord, I am not fluent in English. How I will write a book in English?"

"When you went to college in Brazil, did you speak Portuguese?" he asked.

"No," I answered.

"What happened?"

"You taught me to read and to write that language," I replied. "I trusted you. I went to college and I finished with success."

"I am really proud of your answers," he said. "What happened in Brazil was the preparation for this job. Now go and trust me again. I will be with you and you will have my reward."

At that moment I felt scared and asked myself, who am I that God has chosen me to deliver his message? I have faced many challenges in my life, but this one was huge and far beyond my abilities. At the same time I was excited because I had an assignment from God. I wasn't unemployed anymore. God had a plan for my life. But my mind was full of questions: Who am I to write a book for God? Where and how to start? Who will believe that God has spoken to me? Then I heard the voice of God say, "Why do you scare and torture yourself with those questions? It is not your message, it is mine. You are a simple messenger. The only thing you have to do is deliver the message faithfully. Trust me, I will be with you and you will be fine."

I knew it was the voice of God and decided to obey, to trust, and to give myself to God so he could fulfill his purpose within my life. I am not special, but he chose me to be an instrument in his hand. I could not believe how quickly the three days passed. I said to the Lord, "I don't want to go back into that world anymore; it hurt me badly."

Then he said, "That was before. Now I will be with you and my presence will be around you and your family. Just go and do what I am asking you to do. Trust me and be courageous. Do not be afraid, for I will be with you to guide you." At the end of the third day, I left that house completely renewed and went back to my home, ready to obey God. I had a purpose to fulfill and knew that would be my priority.

After a while, God persuaded me to join a program that consisted of twenty-one days of fasting and prayer led by a wonderful minister of God, Pastor Jetenzen Franklin. I did, and at the end of the fasting, God used him to anoint people, including me. After that anointing, the courage and the inspiration to write came to me, and my mind and ears were clear to hear God's voice and to receive his revelations. Since that Sunday, the restoration has been in my family. God healed and blessed my family in many ways, financially, spiritually, and physically.

I have to thank him for every person he used as an instrument to support me and my family. Money was coming from friends and families members everywhere in the world. People touched by God were supporting us in many ways. God healed my husband and gave him back his hope for the future. I again saw my husband laughing, excited and happy for a new beginning. The past was behind us and the future looked brilliant.

The hand of the Lord was behind everything. God was in control and he kept his promises. While I was writing this book, he took care of my needs and encouraged me to continue in his way. It isn't easy, but I learned to trust and stayed connected to God every second of my life. That season finally passed. Today I understand that bad times in life have a divine purpose. God used that hard season to make us uncomfortable where we were and push us toward our destiny.

We are thankful to God for using hard times to build our faith and make us stronger than ever. After that period of testing I understand the scripture that says, "And we know that all things work together for good to them that love God, to them who are called according to His purpose."[5] God is a good Lord, and I will always sing for him and praise his holy name, for when I was poor and needy, he rescued me.

When I returned home, I told my husband what God had said to me. I saw in his eyes that he didn't believe I would be able to write a book, but he didn't say anything to discourage me. So I decided to not tell anybody about the book and keep it secret. Then when I thought I had finished writing the manuscript, I gave it with excitement to the first person I trusted to read it. The person returned it to me and said the book wasn't ready yet and I had a lot of work to do. I was discouraged, and for weeks I didn't want to touch the manuscript anymore.

---

5   Roman 8:28

One day I was in prayer with one of my friends, filled by the Holy Spirit, when she said, "Sister Ernestine, you have a message from God to all the nations of the world." This time God used her to talk to me. She didn't know that I was writing this book. I was the only one who understood what she was talking about. She described the kind of book I was writing and what was important to write and tell God's people. Through her, God directed my path and reminded me to get back to work. That was what I needed at that time—someone else used by God to confirm that it was God's will for me to write and deliver his message.

After the prayer, my friend said to me, "I don't know if God gave you a message already, but if not, be prepared, because you have a job from God. That message will be delivered to all the nations of the world. Don't search for a job anymore. God will give you a salary." It was wonderful to hear those words of encouragement from my friend. I knew God was speaking through her, and that filled my heart with joy. That day I returned to the manuscript and let the Holy Spirit direct me again.

If you read this book, don't skip any chapters, because the Holy Spirit uses wonderful teaching and amazing stories and illustrations to reveal God's truth. This is a book messenger. I pray that God will help you to understand, and to receive and obey his instructions. It is not by mistake that you have this book in your hand today. God loves you, and he has a plan to save you and give you eternal life. God doesn't want you to miss anything he is preparing for his righteousness at this present moment. Get ready to learn from the Holy Spirit.

It is an honor for me to share my testimony with God's people. May God bless you. This message is for you. It will transform your life, like it transformed mine. Don't miss this opportunity to share it with someone you love and care for.

Chapter 2:

The Beautiful Garden of Eden

And the Lord God planted a garden eastward in Eden, and
there he put the man whom he had formed.

——Genesis 2:8

T o understand why God always sends messengers, and why he has given me this assignment to deliver his message to his people, we have to start from the beginning of everything: when God created man, where he placed him for the first time, and what happened there.

When God created man, he said, "Let us make man in our image, according to our likeness."[6] God planted the Garden of Eden and put in it the man whom he had formed. In the garden, God made grow every tree, good food, and rivers where there was gold and onyx stone. God created there everything that man needed and could enjoy. Man is the important creature that God has made and created to live forever with him. He is God's best friend and has the privilege to live in the mighty presence of God.

God gave man everything: dominion, power, freedom, and his blessing. Man's job was to keep the garden, to dress it, and to enjoy everything that was beautifully made for him. God gave man and woman permission to eat every fruit of the garden. But God prohibited them to eat the fruit of the Tree of Knowledge of Good and Evil. It is written that God said, "Do not eat the fruit of the tree of knowledge of good and evil. If one day you

---

6   Genesis 2:26

eat from it, you will die."[7] God didn't want his best friend to experience the evil side, because he knew how painful it is and that it could lead him to eternal death. Man agreed to obey God and made a covenant of trust with him and promised to stay faithful and obey his instructions.

The fruit prohibited by God contained the knowledge of evil, which wasn't made for mankind. God didn't want any man to end up in the place made for evil-kind. Man has all God's characteristics, including love, mercy, compassion, happiness, and peacefulness. Man was made for happiness and to live forever in the presence of God. Man and woman were happily living in the garden and never had to worry about anything. They had everything they needed and had pure hearts full of God's joy and were freely talking and walking with God every day.

The Devil, who also is Lucifer, was jealous of the friendship between God and man. He had the evil side inside him and was destined already for the place of eternal death. He decided to contaminate the man's race with his evil side. He approached the woman using lies and manipulation and made her believe that he was right and that it was good to eat the prohibited fruit. Then the woman trusted him, ate it, and gave it to her husband. Then both of them broke their covenant of obedience with God and let the evil side enter into their hearts.

For the first time man and woman experienced the ugliness of the evil side of life led by the Devil, who was the first to disobey God. The Devil lost the privilege of being an angel of God and made mankind fall into sin and lose their privilege of living in the Garden of Eden in God's presence. Without holiness, man couldn't see God's face. God by nature is holy, and only holy creatures can approach him and survive. Sin came between mankind and God and separated them. Since the first man opened the door of sin, he was pushed far away from God's face to survive. Now he was divided between good and evil, but the ugly side of the Devil dominated man's heart far from God's presence, and he had become insensitive to God's voice, like a rock. Man's desires continuously inclined toward the evil side.

Man lost the strength, authority, dominion, and power to discern that he had in God's presence. Man slowly became blind minded and couldn't hear God's voice clearly anymore. Without God, man was lost and confused,

---

7   Genesis 2:17

and suffered under the Devil's control that continuously pushes him far from God. God's best friend was completely out of mind and disconnected from his creator. He couldn't trust or hear God's words anymore. Man's spiritual life died and was shut off inside his soul. Something precious was missing inside man, leaving a huge emptiness that he began to fill with false gods, idols, drugs, and alcoholic beverages.

From heaven, God was observing man. He was sad. He had created men to live forever, but they were dying earlier because of their sins. The first people God created lived for a long time. Adam lived 930 years. His son Seth lived 912 years. But when man began to commit horrible sins, the Lord said, "My Spirit will not remain with mankind forever, because they are corrupt. Their days will be 120 years."[8] Living longer is a blessing from God to people who honor him by following his instructions.

Time after time, and generation after generation, the people on Earth continued to commit acts of violence and act even more evil. When the Lord saw that man's wickedness was widespread on the Earth and his mind was corrupt by thinking evil at all times, the Bible says in Genesis, "God regretted that He had made man on the Earth."[9] God decided to wipe him off the face of the Earth by using a huge flood. God appeared to a man named Noah and charged him to announce his decision to all people. If they believed him and changed their evil ways, he would protect them against the flood.

But people didn't take God's message seriously. Only Noah believed God and was found righteous in God's eye. He was God's first messenger and blameless among his contemporaries. He obeyed God's instructions and made an ark in which God protected him and his family against the flood. God established a covenant with Noah that he would protect him and his family and all kinds of animals that Noah took with him in the ark. When Noah and his family came out of the ark after the flood, God blessed them and said, "Be fruitful and multiply and fill the Earth."[10] God promised that he would never again curse the ground because of man's sins, even though man's inclination is evil.

---

8   Genesis 6:3
9   Genesis 6:7
10   Genesis 9:1

A long time after the flood, other people living in Sodom and Gomorrah were acting evil in God's eyes, sinning greatly against the Lord. Then the Lord said, "The outcry against Sodom and Gomorrah is immense, and their sin is extremely serious."[11] Then God decided to destroy those two cities. Only one man named Lot was saved because of prayers and supplication of his uncle Abraham to God.

When the angels of God went to save Lot, they asked him to advise his friends and relatives that the cities were about to be destroyed. As messenger, Lot went to his sons-in-law and friends and advised them what was about to happen. He tried hard to persuade them to leave the town with him, but they thought he was joking and didn't believe him and ignored his advice. Then the angels of the Lord took Lot, his wife, and his two daughters outside of the city and instructed them not to look back and to run to the mountains. Lot's wife did not follow the instructions; she looked back and became a pillar of salt. The Lord rained burning sulfur on those cities, destroyed them, and erased them from the surface of the Earth.

We have two stories of destruction, one with a flood and other with burning sulfur. We also have two messengers chosen by God to advise people and give them a chance to change their evil ways, but people didn't listen and perished. Those people were destroyed not because of their sins, but because they didn't repent and didn't take God's message seriously. God is merciful and slow to anger for those people who change their evil ways and ask for mercy.

The consequence of sin is death. But God has the power to forgive and to save people who acknowledge him and cry for his help. God always gives opportunities to people to repent before he leaves them to destruction. He always sends his angels or messengers to advise and to prepare people to repent, to change, and to choose his good side of life. God will always save the righteous and leave the wicked to destruction.

God doesn't look at people as majorities or minorities. If many people agree to practice evil and don't repent from their sins, they will perish. If only one man repents and cries for God's help, God will rescue only him. God does not judge the majority but will judge every man as an individual. God looks at the intention of men's hearts and reads people from inside.

---

11 Genesis 18:20

If he finds innocence, men will be saved, and if he finds guilt, they will be given a chance to repent before he lets them go to destruction. God said through the prophet Jeremiah, "But I, the Lord, search all hearts and examine secret motives. I give all people their due rewards, according to what their actions deserve."[12] God is a just judge. He judges people fairly. One person saved by God has his power, and he and God are the majority. God makes people powerful and strong. The prophet Elisha said to his servant who was scared of troops, horses, and chariots of the enemy, "Don't be afraid, for there are more on our side than on theirs."[13] With God by his side, the prophet Elisha was strong and powerful. He won many battles.

The will of God has never been to destroy anybody, but when a man turns against God's goodness by choosing evil ways and refuses to repent, he has to pay the consequences. Man is responsible for his choices. God said, "But if your heart turns away and you refuse to listen, and if you are drawn away to serve and worship other gods, then I warn you now that you will certainly be destroyed. You will not live a long, good life in the Land."[14] God's anger burned against people who did not obey his instruction, and they were extinguished from the Earth.

God will be always sad and disappointed with man's disobedience and bad choices, but he never gives up on him and never stops loving him and giving him opportunities to escape the destruction. God wants men to reconnect with his light, his goodness, and his power. He wants men to return to his goodness and live a life without suffering. The people who choose God's side are able to feel happiness and peace. God will continue to give people the opportunity to come back to him. In God's hands, people are protected against the Devil and his demons.

If God destroyed wicked people before, he can destroy and erase them again today. If God saved the righteousness people before, he will save and bless them again today. Because of sin, people perish. God always send messages to give people hope and the opportunity to avoid destruction and come back to life. We have to avoid the mistakes made by the elders and choose God's side of life and goodness. With God's presence we have the

---

12   Jeremiah 17:10
13   2 Kings 6:16
14   Deuteronomy 30:17–18

ability to discern good and evil and make wise decisions. God will always reward those who are faithful and obedient. They will always rejoice in the goodness and the rich glory of God forever and ever.

Chapter 3:

The Great Righteous People of God

I will make all my goodness pass before you, and I will call out my name, Yahweh, before you. For I will show mercy to anyone I choose, and I will show compassion to anyone I choose.

—Exodus 34:19

The Tree of Knowledge of Good and Evil made everyone responsible for choosing good or evil. But God gives people all the tools they need to make wise and right decisions and choose the good side of life. God has to choose some people to serve as examples to others, pour his Spirit into them, and reveal himself through them to humanity. Those select people were chosen by the grace of the Lord and not because they were perfect or smart. God has the power to choose whom he wants to fulfill and to accomplish his divine purpose on Earth.

The chosen people have the right to welcome God's calling or to reject it. God equips those who freely accept his calling and follow his instructions with his Spirit, and they are called righteous. God fills them with his power, wisdom, and knowledge and provides for them everything they need to fulfill his purposes. In this chapter we will see how God appeared to some of his chosen people and used them for his glory. God gave them supernatural gifts and used them powerfully. He gave them prosperity, lands, and houses they did not build. He put them in high positions that they never dreamed of reaching and gave them favors and treasures they did not work for.

Abraham is the famous righteous friend of God. God chose him when he was a young man living with his father and his brothers. God appeared to him and asked him to leave his father's house, his relatives, and his land and to go to an unknown land that he would show him. Abraham believed God's promises and went to an unknown country as the Lord asked him. He took with him his wife and his nephew Lot.

Because Abraham obeyed God's instructions, God made a covenant with him and said, "I will give this land to your offspring, from the brook of Egypt to the Euphrates."[15] And God gave him this promise: "I will make you into a great nation, I will bless you, I will make your name great, and you will be a blessing."[16] God by his grace decided to make Abraham and his wife, Sarah, the first parents of a new family of righteousness people of God. Those who chose the goodness of God and obeyed and followed his paths would be members of Abraham's family. This new family would be empowered by God to defeat sin and evil. A great nation of righteousness would be born through Abraham.

Abraham became a wealthy and influential man of his time because of God's blessing. His entire household was covered by God's presence. Later on, Abraham decided to separate from his nephew Lot because of the quarreling between their herdsmen. Abraham told Lot it was time for them to go their separate ways, and he gave Lot the right to choose first where he wanted to go. Abraham said, "If you go to the left, I will go to the right; if you go to the right, I will go to the left."[17] Abraham was a peaceful man. He didn't want quarreling in the family. He needed peace and quiet surrounding him to freely connect with God. He wanted his nephew to understand that although he loved him, God was not welcome in a place where there was no peace. Abraham's priority was God's presence. He valued that more than anything. To have peace with God, he decided to let go of his nephew. Then Lot chose to live in the valley of Jordan, near Sodom and Gomorrah. That place looked good and nice to Lot; it seemed to him to be a wonderful place to live. But for God, that place was horrible, violent, and full of all kinds of sins.

---

15   Genesis 15:18
16   Genesis 17:4
17   Genesis 13:9

Lot freely made a wrong choice. First, he couldn't accept the separation between himself and his uncle. Lot had the honor of living with an anointed man of God and had made a fortune because of Abraham's covenant of blessing with God. Lot had to find a way to solve the quarrel between the herdsmen and keep peace in the household. By being proud, he accepted the separation from his uncle Abraham and forgot that he was officially separating himself from the blessing and anointing of God.

Secondly, Lot made his choice without consulting God. He didn't search for God's will for his life. He made his choice based on how beautiful those cities looked from the outside. He didn't know how those cities looked inside, and for that he needed God's advice and warnings. Those cities looked nice and perfect, but inside they were dangerous, full of criminals, immoral, and about to be destroyed by God. Lot went there and had very painful experiences. He had to be rescued from trouble by his uncle many times. When God sent his angels to erase the cities of Sodom and Gomorrah off the map, Lot and his family were saved because of Abraham's supplications to God. He cried to God and asked him to protect and rescue Lot and his family.

There is one woman named Ruth in the Bible who had to choose to leave her mother-in-law rather than stay with her. Her mother-in-law one day says to her, "Go back to your home; my life is much too bitter for you."[18] But Ruth responded to her, "Do not persuade me to leave you or go back and not follow you. For wherever you go, I will go, and wherever you live, I will live; your people will be my people and your God will be my God."[19] Naomi, the mother-in-law, was a poor widow with nothing to offer, but Ruth decided to obey the voice inside her that persuaded her not to abandon that poor widow. She did not expect anything from her mother-in-law, but to honor the memory of her husband, she decided to take care of her. She freely chose to stay and go with her wherever she decided to live. God rewarded her for her faithfulness, her humility, and her commitment to serve and help a poor widow. Later she married a wealthy man from her mother-in-law's land and her name is written in the bloodline of the greatest kings of Israel.

18   Ruth 1:15
19   Ruth 1:16

The Lot and Ruth stories teach us to not judge people or things for how they look or are represented from the outside. Only God knows the inner side of everything. Things may look good and nice from the outside, but from the inside they may be ugly, evil, and dangerous. For that reason, we have to consult God before making any decision. He knows better. It is written in the book of the prophet Samuel, "The Lord doesn't see things the way you see them. People judge by outward appearance, but the Lord looks at the heart."[20]Many times people make wrong choices, and that pushes them far from God's will. We cannot ignore God's advice and instruction and expect to succeed. This was the case with Lot: he lost everything he owned, even his wife, and had to start all over again. For every wrong choice people make, a bad consequence is attached to it. We don't have to learn the hard way as Lot did. It's time to avoid Lot's mistakes and consult God for everything.

Abraham made God the center and the priority of his life. He trusted him and couldn't do anything without his approval. Abraham understood these principles: God's approval is the key to success in every area, and although things and people don't last forever, God does. Abraham walked side by side with God. He knew that without God he couldn't have anything. Only God has the power and strength to save and to bless people. It is written in the book of Zachariah, "This is what the Lord says to Zerubbabel: it is not by force or by strength, but by my Spirit, says the Lord of heaven's armies."[21] It is the Spirit of the Lord that makes a difference in people's lives and makes everything possible.

Abraham's wife, Sarah, was barren, meaning she could not have children. But God promised Abraham that he would be the father of many. By faith, Abraham believed and trusted God. He and Sarah were old and getting on in years and the process of waiting was painful for Sarah and led her to make a wrong decision. Sarah asked her husband to have a child with her servant, and Abraham did it. That was a shortcut and not in God's plan for them. Impatient people always take shortcuts, which give temporary pleasure but can turn into a nightmare in the future.

Waiting for God's promise may take a long time and seem impossible, but God is in control of time and circumstances. The word *impossible*

---

20 1 Samuel 16:7
21 Zachariah 4:6

doesn't exist in God's vocabulary. Sarah had passed the age of child bearing when the angel of the Lord came and announced that she would have a son the next year. When Sarah heard it, she laughed and said, "Can I really have a baby when I'm old?"[22]

The angel of the Lord responded, "Is anything impossible for the Lord?"[23] Abraham was a faithful man; he trusted God, and God accomplished what he had promised to him.

It is written, "Then Abraham waited patiently, and he received what God had promised."[24] It took twenty-five years for God to accomplish his promise to Abraham and Sarah that they would have a biological son. God knew when the perfect time was. It may look like a long time for people, but for God it was the right time. God's answers to prayer never came early or late but at the perfect time. Sarah became pregnant and bore a son in her old age, and they named him Isaac. Abraham became the father of righteousness because of his faith and his unconditional love for God.

Another great righteous man of God was Moses. God chose him to deliver his people from slavery in Egypt. Moses was an Israelite born into a slave household, but by God's grace, he was raised by Pharaoh's daughter as a prince in the palace. Moses knew he came from Israelite roots and felt inside the desire to fight for justice and deliver his people from slavery. But one day he made a wrong decision: he killed an Egyptian who was biting one of his people.

When the secret came out, Moses was exposed, and he knew Pharaoh would kill him. He decided to run to save his life. Moses's future was uncertain outside Egypt. He didn't know where to go and what to do far from the palace and his people, but God directed his path to a strange Land of Median, where Moses became a shepherd. He thought his dream was ended and God was punishing him for his wrong decision. Moses conformed himself to the reality of the new land and decided to survive and do whatever job he could find.

God did not change his plan for Moses's life. Moses may have given up on his dream, but God did not. Moses was going through the process of being shaped and prepared by the Lord to become a liberator of Israel's

---

22 Genesis 18:10
23 Genesis 18:14
24 Hebrews 6:15

people. God, on purpose, let Moses experience the pain of forced labor. He learned to be patient, to love, and to lead the sheep. Moses learned humility, endurance, self-control, and patience. When Moses was ready, God appeared to him and sent him back into Egypt to deliver his people. Through Moses, God showed his mighty power through signs, wonders, and demonstrations of supernatural power that never occur on Earth.

Another famous righteousness man of God was King David. David was neglected and ignored by his father and his brothers. His father could not remember him when the prophet of God came to his house to anoint him. God knew David, and he poured his Spirit of wisdom, worship, and power in him. David was chosen and anointed by God's grace at a young age to become King of Israel. But before he became king, David had to run, to hide, and to patiently and faithfully wait for God's time to reign as king. God rewarded him for his patience and his faithfulness, and David became a powerful and wise king than any king the earth had ever known.

These people were ordinary people elected and chosen by God's grace to reveal God's characteristics of goodness, love, and power. It is written, "So it is God who decides to show mercy. We can neither choose it nor work for it."[25] What made these elect people special was their friendship with God. They were faithful men of God, and they loved, worshipped, and obeyed God's law. God chose them to reveal his names, his character, his personalities, his mercy, his grace, his goodness, and his mighty power to humanity.

God is a sovereign. He chooses whom he wants, he gives to whom he wants, and he blesses when he wants. He wants people to know him, and through his chosen people he reveals himself. It is written in Romans, "But before they were born, before they had done anything good or bad. God chooses them according to his own purposes; He calls people not according to their good or bad works."[26] God elects people according to his own purposes and pours inside them his Spirit to manifest his own glory.

All these chosen friends of God have something in common: they said yes to God's calling and God's ways and committed themselves to serving him. They all obeyed, believed, and trusted God. God rewarded them,

---

25   Romans 9:16
26   Romans 9:11–12

blessed them, and gave them a peaceful life. He filled them with wisdom and knowledge and gave them his mighty power. He made them rich and influential figures—leaders, prophets, judges, and kings—and their names will be known forever.

All these extraordinary life stories are written in the Bible as examples to teach us and encourage us to love, to obey, and to serve God. Being a righteous person is a privilege and given by grace from God. Anyone who wants a better life of peace and prosperity has to say yes to God's ways and decide to obey and trust God.

Chapter 4:

The Rescue of the Israelites in Egypt

So I have come down to rescue them from the power of the Egyptians and lead them out of Egypt into their own fertile and spacious land.

——Exodus 3:8

This chapter is very important because it shows that God can do anything to save and deliver his children from the hand of the enemy. This chapter will give us confidence in God's love and power. It will help people know that God has the power to end pain, misery, suffering, and the slavery of sin. The purpose of this chapter is to remind people that God has rescued his people before and will do it again. The slavery and the rescue of the Israelites represent the slavery of the sin of humanity and the divine intervention from God to rescue his people from the power of the Devil.

The Israelites are the descendants of Abraham. They immigrated into Egypt because of famine in their land. God advised Abraham a long time ago and said to him, "Know this for certain: Your offspring will be strangers in a land that does not belong to them; they will be enslaved and oppressed 400 years."[27] Before they went into Egypt, God prepared Joseph, the son of Jacob, to go before his people. His brothers sold him as a slave, but God turned his situation into a blessing and made him an influential personality in the land of Egypt. Joseph said to his brothers,

---

27   Genesis 15:13

"But don't be upset, and don't be angry with yourselves for selling me to this place. It was God who sent me here ahead of you to preserve your lives."[28]As long as Joseph was alive, his people were welcomed in Egypt and treated with dignity and honor. But after his death, the new Pharaoh reduced the Israelites to slavery because he was afraid and jealous of their prosperity. He said to the Egyptian people, "Look, the Israelite people are more numerous and powerful than we are. Let us deal shrewdly with them; otherwise they will multiply, and if war breaks out, they may join our enemies."[29] Then Pharaoh and the Egyptians assigned taskmasters over the Israelites to oppress them with forced labor.

They worked the Israelites ruthlessly and made their lives bitter with difficult labor making brick and mortar, and in all kinds of fieldwork. They ruthlessly imposed all this work on them. The Israelites were forced to live in poverty and misery. For years, Pharaoh reduced the Israelites to slavery. They didn't have power, goals, or purpose. They had to satisfy only the desires of the Egyptians. They were living in the shadow of their masters. The Israelites suffered under the brutality of the Egyptians' power. Slavery is not always about hard work; it can also be mental, physical, spiritual, and emotional.

For years they cried to God for help. They always knew that their fathers had a powerful God who could help and could deliver them from the Egyptians. After they accomplished 430 years of slavery in Egypt, God appeared to Moses in a flame of fire within a bush. Then God called out to him from the bush and said to him, "I am Yahweh, the Lord. I appeared to Abraham, to Isaac and to Jacob as El-Shaddai, God Almighty, but I did not reveal my name, Yahweh, to them."[30] He said to him, "I have come down to rescue my people from the power of the Egyptians and bring them from that land, to a good and spacious land, a land flowing with milk and honey."[31]God heard the cry of the Israelites, had compassion for them, and decided to come down and rescue them as he had promised to Abraham. Moses was eighty years old when God appeared to him and sent him to deliver the Israelites from the Egyptians' power. Moses couldn't believe

---

28 Genesis 45:5
29 Exodus 1:9
30 Exodus 6:3
31 Exodus 3:8

that God would use him again. He hesitated to obey God and gave him excuses and reasons why he wasn't the right person. Moses asked questions like What if they ask me your name? What if they don't listen to me? And what if they don't believe me?

Those questions reveal the state of Moses's character at that time. He didn't have enough confidence in God or in himself. God had to build his confidence by revealing his power. Moses said to God, "Please, Lord, send someone else, because I am slow and hesitant in speech."[32] At his age, Moses was thinking about retirement, but God had another plan for his life. Moses had a hard time forgetting about his weaknesses and focusing on God's plan. But God did not give up on him.

The Lord's anger burned against him and God asked him, "Who made the human mouth? Who makes him mute or deaf, seeing or blind? Is it not I, the Lord? Now go! I will help you speak and I will teach you what to say. And your brother Aaron will be your spokesman."[33] God wanted Moses to know that he was mighty God, the creator of everything, and that Moses didn't have to worry about anything when God was by his side. God had to work on Moses's character and build up his self-esteem and reassure him that everything would be all right with him in charge. God repeated over and over to Moses, "I will certainly be with you, I will help you, and I will teach you what to do."[34] When people focus more on their own imperfections and weakness than on God's mighty power, they fail, because they are putting limits on God. Moses had to know God, trust him, and give himself completely to him. When Moses stopped limiting God's power and focused more on God's instructions, ignoring his own imperfections and his weakness by trusting God's words, then God performed supernatural things through him. Moses's story teaches us that God can use anybody at any age to fulfill his purpose.

Most of the time, people who refuse to serve God are miserable. They don't succeed at anything they try to do, and frustration is created in their life. They become depressed, sick, and empty inside because they are not in their divine purpose of life. God has a divine purpose for every living creature that he made. Everyone has to find God's purpose for his or her

---

32 Exodus 4:10
33 Exodus 4:11
34 Exodus 4:12

life and let him have control. Only in God's will and God's ways will people have success, peace, joy, balance, and satisfaction.

God said to Moses, "The Israelites' cry for help has come to me, and I have also seen the way the Egyptians are oppressing them. Therefore, go. I am sending you to Pharaoh so that you may lead my people, the Israelites, out to Egypt."[35] Moses went back to Pharaoh's house and asked him to let his people go to worship God on the mountain of the Lord. God used Moses powerfully before Pharaoh, and he honored him before the Israelites. With God's Spirit and power, Moses delivered his people from Egypt.

When the Israelites were leaving Egypt, God let them take the long way through the wilderness. They didn't have a map or any directions. God was their map, and they had to trust him and let him lead them. His presence was inside a pillar of cloud during the day and a pillar of fire by night, so they could travel day and night. Wherever the cloud was lifted above the tent, the Israelites would set out; at the place where the cloud stopped, there the Israelites camped. At the Lord's command they camped, and moved out.

In the wilderness, life for the Israelites was hard and difficult. God chose the hard way through the wilderness to test their faith and teach them not to depend on their own strength but only on God's provision and strength. God provided them with water, bread, and anything they needed to survive. He wanted his people to experience his mighty power and learn to make him their only source. God was taking out the slavery mentality inside their minds by transforming and renewing their character and made them worthy to live in the new place that he prepared for them to enjoy.

God had to work on their behavior and help them build their confidence after being slaves for a long time. God had to teach them to appreciate and enjoy freedom. He gave them new laws and commands to learn and obey. God sharpened them, and taught them endurance, perseverance, and self-defense. He had to reestablish their dignity and empower them. Slaves don't have purpose to pursue; God had to give them a purpose, which was to reach the Promised Land no matter the barriers and giants in their way.

---

35 Exodus 3:9–10

After the Israelites left Egypt, Pharaoh and his officials changed their minds and decided to chase after them. Pharaoh gathered his army, his chariot, his horses, and his powerful-looking weapons and went after them to bring them back to Egypt. The Israelites didn't have any weapons or an army, but they had the presence of God and Moses and his staff. As Pharaoh and his army approached, the Israelites panicked and cried out to the Lord. The angel of God, who was going in front of the Israelites, moved and went behind them. The pillar of cloud moved from in front of them and stood behind them, between the Egyptian forces and the Israelites. Then God asked Moses to stretch out his staff over the sea. Moses obeyed God, and waters covered Pharaoh's chariots and his entire army. None of them survived. The Lord with his mighty power fought for the Israelites and gave them victory against the enemy.

The Israelites witnessed God's demonstration of power and glory through Moses in Egypt and in the wilderness. But when life was tough and they didn't have what they wanted, and when they had to fight against other people in their passage to the Promised Land, they rebelled, argued, and complained to Moses and were not grateful and faithful to God. Then God said to Moses, "How long will these people despise me? How long will they not trust in me despite all the signs I have performed among them?"[36] The trip in the wilderness took forty years because of the Israelites' ungrateful attitude. God had said to them, "You will bear the consequences of your sins forty years based on the number of the forty days that you scouted the land, a year for each day. You will know my displeasure. I, the Lord, have spoken. I swear that I will do this to the entire evil community that has conspired against me. They will come to an end in the wilderness, and there they will die."[37] God decided that only those under twenty years old would enter the land he promised to their fathers. Only two men from the older generation, who were faithful and had trusted him, continued with the new generation to the Promised Land. Because of God's promise to Abraham, all the descendants of Abraham had to inherit the privilege of living in the Promised Land. But their bad behavior and unfaithful character made them lose their privilege of getting

---

36   Numbers 14:26–30
37   Numbers 14:33

to the Promised Land. They didn't trust and had disobeyed the God of their fathers Abraham, Isaac, and Jacob.

Because of their unfaithful and ungrateful hearts, they had a disastrous ending. They perished in the wildness. What a sad ending. It is written in the book of the prophet Jeremiah, "For I know the plans I have for you, says the Lord: they are plans for good and not for disaster, to give you a future and hope."[38] God had a good plan for them, but they had to trust and obey his commands to see that plan come to pass in their life. When God is in charge, people have to let him lead even when troubles come. God is able to intervene by his power, and he will deliver and rescue his people as he has promised.

God chose the Israelites to serve as examples for us today. Through them, God revealed his name, his personality, his power, his love, and his plan for humanity. The Israelites' stories are God's stories also, and they help people know and understand God. In the book of Romans it is written, "They are the people of Israel, chosen to be God's adopted children. God reveals his glory to them."[39] The Israelites were chosen by God to be his people and to reveal him to humanity.

God will rescue his people today as he did in the past. He will come down to rescue his people who cry under the slavery of sin the same way he did in Egypt. The Devil and his army will perish in the same way Pharaoh and his army perished in the Red Sea. It is written in the book of the prophet Isaiah, "What sorrow awaits those who look to Egypt for help, trusting their horses, chariots, and charioteers and depending on the strength of human armies instead of looking to the Lord, the Holy One of Israel …When the Lord raises his fist against them, those who help will stumble and those being helped will fall. They will all fall down and die together."[40]

---

38   Jeremiah 29:11
39   Romans 9:4
40   Isaiah 31:1–3

Chapter 5:

The Shadow of Sacrificial Love

And God said to Abraham: take now your son, your only son Isaac, who you love and get into the land of Moriah and offer him there for a burnt offering upon one of the mountains which I will show you.

—*Genesis 22:2*

It is difficult for people to dominate their weak and evil sides and make right choices by their own strength. More people are corrupt, blind, and perishing in sins. The Devil has turned people's hearts, making them insensitive, aggressive, and rebellious, unable to distinguish what's right and good. God sentenced the Devil already and made a place where he will be thrown for eternity. The apostle John saw in the book of Revelation that place called hell and wrote, "Then the Devil, who had deceived people, was thrown into the fiery lake of burning sulfur, joining the beast and the false prophet. There they will be tormented day and night forever and ever."[41] Hell is the place prepared for the Devil, his demons, and those who freely make the choice to follow them. They were thrown alive there for eternal suffering. That place is the horrible place for horrible creatures and was made just for them. The Devil is Lucifer, an angel of God. One day he said to himself, "I will ascend to heaven; I will set up my throne above the stars of God. I will sit on the mount of the god's assembly. I will ascend above the highest cloud; I will make myself like the most High."[42] He

---

41 Revelation 20:10
42 Isaiah 14:13

wanted to be equal to God. He was jealous and proud, and God expelled him and threw him down to Earth, where he is reigning, waiting for the end of time. One day he will lose his strength and will be thrown into the lake of burning sulfur, where he will burn forever for all he has done.

God doesn't want people to join the Devil in hell because it wasn't designed for people. God did not appoint people to wrath. The Devil is a liar and never wants people to know the truth. Here on Earth, with great fury, the Devil has brought curses upon people. He introduced sin to people, and man's mind has been blinded by him and bad things such as sickness, diseases, earthquakes, natural disasters, wickedness, and all kind of curses that have occurred on the Earth where people live under his constant influence. That hasn't ever been God's will for his people.

God has brought his people too far to give up on them. He couldn't stop loving them even when they were choosing the evil side and being unfaithful. He has to make a plan to rescue their blind hearts, give them strength, and help them discern correctly what's right and wrong. God has to empower his people and teach them to resist the Devil and overcome fear and blindness. As a good father with unconditional love, God planned to fight and deliver his children from the Devil's influence and dominion.

Nothing could separate God from his children, even the Devil. God said, "I thought to myself, I would love to treat you as my own children! I wanted nothing more than to give you this beautiful land, the finest possession in the world. I looked forward to you calling me Father; I wanted you never to turn from me."[43] God's love is powerful. He kindly intends to forgive people for their sins and wrongdoings and give them hope and a good future.

In secret, God elaborated a salvation plan for his children. For years, he revealed some clues of his plan through his people. The first clue is found in his friendship with Abraham when he asked him to offer his son, Isaac, as sacrifice. We learned earlier how Abraham waited for a long time to have Isaac, the promised child from God. But God tested Abraham and asked him to sacrifice his son. God had never asked for a human sacrifice. Abraham had always offered God animals for sacrifice. But when God asked him for his son, he did not question it or refuse him his son. He

---

43   Jeremiah 3:19

knew God, and even though he didn't understand God's intentions, he decided to obey and trust him.

Abraham showed faith and confidence in God. He took his son and went to the place that God had showed him. He built the altar, arranged the wood, bound Isaac, placed him on the altar on top of the wood, and was ready to reach for the knife to slaughter him for God. Isaac could have screamed or tried to escape, thinking that his father was crazy. Instead he let Abraham bind him without complaining. But the Angel of the Lord called Abraham and stopped him from killing Isaac. God provided a ram for him to offer as burnt offering in Isaac's place.

What does the ram represent? It is a symbol of divine provision from heaven. God revealed himself to Abraham as Jehovah Jireh, God who provides. The ram was an offering given by God as a sacrifice to clean and sanctify the entire world. By testing Abraham, God was proving Abraham's love for him. Abraham didn't hesitate to offer his only son as a sacrifice to show his commitment and his unconditional love to God. Isaac's story is a clue that reveals that God, because he loves his children, will not hesitate to give in sacrifice his beloved son as a burnt offering to redeem people from sins. God will never refuse to give his only son in sacrifice for the love of his people.

Abraham's love symbolizes God's love. He gave his only son for sacrifice to show his faithfulness. God's love is infinite, unconditional, and profound. Sometimes we don't realize how precious we are to God. It is good to remember how God loves us and that he will always be among us to help, to protect, and to rescue. He has a wonderful plan for our lives. Nothing can separate us from God's love unless we turn ourselves against him and reject his love and his help. God cannot force our will. We have freely decided to receive his offer of love and help.

The second clue is found in God's recommendation to Moses to use the blood as a symbol of covenant, for protection, and for the forgiveness of their sins. It is written, "Then Moses took the blood from the basins and splattered it over the people declaring: Look, this blood confirms the covenant the Lord has made with you in giving you these instructions."[44] God was revealing that the blood has to be the symbol of covenant between God and people.

---

44   Exodus 24:8

One night at an overnight campsite, the Lord confronted Moses and sought to put him to death, but Moses's wife, Zipporah, took a flint, cut off her son's foreskin, and threw it at Moses's feet. When the Lord saw the blood, he let him live.[45] When God saw the innocent blood of a child, he let Moses live. God showed the importance and the power in the blood of an innocent male. That blood saved Moses's life.

In Egypt, God told the Israelites to choose an unblemished animal, a year-old male lamb or goat, slaughter it, and take its blood and put it on the two doorposts and lintel of their houses. The Lord said to them, "The blood on the house where you are staying will be a distinguishing mark for you. When I see the blood, I will pass over you. No plague will be among you to destroy you when I strike the land of Egypt."[46] The blood on their doors distinguished them from the Egyptians and served as a protective mark. God didn't see people behind the doors, but he saw the blood of an innocent lamb, knew the people behind the doors were Israelites, and spared their lives.

God made a covenant and protected his people and forgave their sins through the blood of an unblemished lamb. Without that blood, there is no salvation and there is no forgiveness. The blood of an innocent lamb sanctified and protected God's people from the destruction. The blood of innocence covered people's sin and made them holy before God. Through that blood they could reach God and hear his voice.

The grace of God was with the Israelites because of his covenant with Abraham, Isaac, and Jacob. God talked and revealed his salvation plan through his prophets years before in the Old Testament, which is foreshadow of what is to come for real. It was announced in advance that the Lamb of God will come and his blood has to be spilled to sanctify, redeem, and protect people from the Devil and hell.

We have learned from this first part that

- God has a wonderful plan of salvation for his people.
- God allowed the wicked to be destroyed and saved the righteous.
- The elect people are called and chosen only by God's grace to fulfill his purpose.

---

45 Exodus 4:24
46 Exodus 12:23

- When people cry for God's help with a sincere heart, he will show up to rescue them. He is faithful and a refuge in time of need and trouble.
- God never gives up on his people even when they are unfaithful. He will always give them another chance to repent and get back to right paths.

PART TWO:

DIVINE INTERVENTION

Chapter 6:

Prophesies about the Messiah

Everything I prophesied has come true, and now I will prophesy again. I will tell you the future before it happens.
——Isaiah 42:9

Through the prophets, God revealed and sent messages about the coming of the Messiah. As God provided a divine ram to Abraham to be sacrificed, God promised to provide a divine lamb from heaven to be sacrificed and set his people free. The Lamb would take the punishment of people onto himself and would pay with his life as offering for sin. The Lord's salvation plan would prosper in his hands.

The prophets of God prophesied about the Lamb of God, also called the Messiah, decades before he came. They wrote about his birth, mission, suffering, death, and resurrection. The prophet Isaiah wrote, "The plan of God will succeed only by His hand. The Messiah will justify many, will save many; will carry their iniquities; and He will bear their sins. Only He was found holy to intercede for them before the throne of God." Through the prophet Isaiah, God said, "I, the Lord, have called you to demonstrate my righteousness. I will take you by the hand and guard you, and I will give you to my people, Israel, as a symbol of my covenant with them."[47]God spoke through the prophet and said, "And I will give you shepherds after my own heart, who will guide you with knowledge and understanding."[48]About his birth, it was written, "The virgin will

---

47   Isaiah 42:6
48   Jeremiah 3:15

conceive, have a son, and name him Immanuel"[49] and "For a child will be born for us, a son will be given to us, and the government will be on His shoulders. He will be named Wonderful, Counselor, Mighty God, Eternal Father, and Prince of Peace … He will reign on the throne of David and over his kingdom, to establish and sustain it with justice and righteousness from now and forever. The zeal of the Lord of Hosts will accomplish this."[50]About his wisdom, the prophet said, "Then a shoot will grow from the stump of Jesse, and a branch from his roots will bear fruit. The Spirit of the Lord will rest on Him: a Spirit of wisdom and understanding, a Spirit of counsel and strength, a Spirit of knowledge and of the fear of the Lord."[51]This is what was prophesied about his suffering: "He grew up before Him like a young plant and like a root out of dry ground. He had no form or splendor that we should look at Him, no appearance that we should desire Him. He was despised and rejected by men, a man of suffering who knew what sickness was. He was like one people turned away from; He was despised, and we didn't value Him. Yet He Himself bore our sickness, and He carried our pains; but we in turn regarded Him stricken, struck down by God, and afflicted. But He was pierced because of our transgressions, crushed because of our iniquities; punishment for our peace was on Him, and we are healed by His wounds."[52]About his death and resurrection, it was written, "Now the Lord had arranged for a great fish to swallow Jonah. And Jonah was inside the fish for three days and three nights." Who can be eaten by a fish and after three days and three nights come back to life? The fish symbolizes the ground that cannot hold the Messiah for more than three days and three nights. Jonah said, "I called to you from the land of dead, and you heard me!"[53] Jonah was chosen as the symbol of the death and resurrection of the Messiah.

Prophecies are very important. They are proof of God's faithfulness, wisdom, power, and knowledge. They reveal what is to come with details and precision. God's prophecies have to be fulfilled because God's word is the truth and is real. When the Messiah was to come, the angel of the Lord came to Joseph, who was engaged to Mary, the virgin chosen by the grace

---

49   Isaiah 7:14
50   Isaiah 9:6–7
51   Isaiah 11:1–2
52   Isaiah 53:2–5
53   Jonah 2:2b

of God to carry the baby, and said to him, "Don't be afraid to take her as your wife. She will give birth to a son, and you are to name Him Jesus, because He will save His people from their sins."[54]Joseph and Mary didn't expect to be chosen as the parents of the Messiah, and they didn't plan to have a baby because they weren't married yet. But God had a plan for their lives by his grace, and that was the perfect time for God. The Messiah was conceived by the power of God. The divine power of God came to the Virgin Mary and she became pregnant. God took his holy seed and planted it inside Mary's womb. God's seed grew and was born through Mary. His name is Jesus Christ, the son of the living God.

He came to Earth to empower God's people and deliver them from the darkness. The salvation was fulfilled by him. He brought light and joy to the Earth and reconnected people with God. He brought heavenly life to Earth. Jesus was the answer to the prayer and the cry of God's children for help and freedom. The Messiah is a symbol of the covenant between God and people. The coming of the Messiah Jesus was divine intervention and the most important event that has happened on Earth. Jesus Christ is the hope of sinners and the joy of God's children.

The angel of the Lord said to the shepherds, "I proclaim to you good news of great joy that will be for all the people: today a Savior, who is Messiah the Lord, was born in the city of David."[55] Suddenly there was a multitude of the heavenly host with the angel, praising God and saying, "Glory to God in the highest heaven and peace on Earth to people he favors."[56]When the chosen parents, Joseph and Mary, brought the child Jesus to the temple for his dedication to the Lord, one man of God named Simeon prophesied about him and said, "He will be a light for revelation to the Gentiles and glory to the Israel people."[57] The Messiah grew with exceptional power, and at age twelve, he began his ministry by teaching and demonstrating God's power. Jesus changed the course of history and brought hope, peace, joy, and freedom to the captive, proclaiming the years of the Lord's favor. People were amazed by the gracious words that

---

54   Matthew 1:20
55   Luke 2:10
56   Luke 2:14
57   Luke 2:32

came from his mouth. He knew the scriptures and explained them with a passion and wisdom they had never witnessed before.

Jesus the Messiah brought light to the world and woke up people's minds, rebuilding their confidence in the word of God. People's spiritual eyes were opened by his exceptional wisdom and power. People worshipped God for his faithfulness and his power through Jesus. Through him, people were healed, renewed, and empowered. Whoever was in touch with Jesus had to be transformed and never looked the same. Jesus changes people from bad to good, from worst to better, and from nobody to somebody.

Christianity is not a religion; it is the only way to receive God's forgiveness and power to overcome an evil mind and reconnect to the high power of God. Jesus is the only savior. He is the ram provided by God to be sacrificed for the people's freedom. He brought holiness, peace, and blessing to the Earth. His holy blood saves, protects, and redeems people. Christianity brings the message of hope, forgiveness, and peace to humanity. Jesus said, "I am the light of the world. If you follow me, you won't have to walk in darkness, because you will have the light that leads to life."[58] Any person and any profession need Jesus. For doctors, he is the great physician. For the sick, he is the healer. For teachers, he is the great teacher. For judges, he is the just judge. For photographers, he is the image of the invisible God. For sinners, he is the forgiver. For the poor, he is their hope and their justice. It is impossible for people to succeed without Jesus's help. Only he has the strength that people need to overcome the Devil. It is written, "For I can do everything through Christ, who gives me strength."[59] He is the plenitude of God in everything, and he is everything for everybody. He teaches, he helps, he heals, he forgives, and he saves. No one can survive the Earth's challenges without Jesus. He is what people need and seek. He is the solution to man's failures.

When people receive the Son of God, the light comes upon their lives and the forces of darkness lose their strength upon them. In the book of Romans it is written, "If you confess with your mouth that Jesus is the Lord and believe in your heart that God raised Him from the dead, you will be saved."[60] We have to confess and declare with our mouths that we

---

58 John 8:12
59 Philippians 4:13
60 Romans 10:9

belong to Jesus. We can't hide Jesus's light. When a day brings his light, the darkness of night has to disappear. People's identities change from night to day when they confess Jesus as Lord and believe that he is the Savior of their lives.

In Jesus Christ people have their names written in the Book of Life and they will have the right to live in the eternity of God. In him, the sinful nature dies and the holy nature arises. Jesus brings a new life. In him people are born again. In a letter to the Romans, the apostle Paul said, "But you are not controlled by your sinful nature. You are controlled by the Spirit if you have the Spirit of God living in you (remember that those who do not have the Spirit of Christ living in them do not belong to Him at all). And Christ lives within you."[61] Jesus came to defeat the evil side, to strengthen people and bring them back to God. He came to encourage those who have tired hands and weak knees. We are not alone anymore. We have a king, a Savior, and an intercessor before the throne of God for days, nights, and eternity. It is written, "He will not crush the weakest reed or put out a flickering candle. He will bring justice to all who have been wronged and He will not falter or lose heart until justice prevails throughout the Earth."[62] The Messiah has the mission to deliver all the nations of the Earth and bring them back to God.

One day people will be judged for not accepting the Messiah's salvation and for rejecting him. Every nation and every tongue now has the opportunity to become righteous and be called Abraham's children through the Messiah's blood. All those who accept Jesus's sacrificial love will become God's children. They will receive peace and forgiveness, and their names will be written in the Book of Life.

The apostle Paul wrote, "And this is God's plan: Both Gentiles and Jews, who believe the Good News, share equally in the riches inherited by God's children. Both are part of the same body, and both enjoy the promises of blessing because they belong to Christ Jesus,"[63] and Jesus said this in the gospel of John: "Now you are my friends, since I have told you everything the Father told me. You didn't choose me. I chose you. I

---

61 Romans 8:9
62 Isaiah 42:3–4
63 Ephesians 3:6

appointed you to go and produce lasting fruit."[64] We are the ambassadors for Jesus Christ in the world. We work for a good cause, which is to bring the message of hope, peace, and salvation to all the nations on Earth.

The prophet Isaiah quotes God as saying, "I, the Lord, have called you for a righteous purpose, and I will hold you by your hand. I will keep you, and I make you a covenant for the people and a light to the nation, in order to open blind eyes, to bring out prisoners from the dungeons, and those sitting in darkness from the prison house."[65] God never gives up on the lost because they are blinded or bad. He never stops loving them and working for their salvation. It is written in First Corinthians, "Love never gives up, never loses faith, is always hopeful, and endures through every circumstance."[66] Prophecies about the Messiah have been fulfilled. He was born from the virgin and lets people contemplate the magnificence power and glory of God. Jesus said, "Spend your energy seeking the eternal life that the Son of Man can give you. For God the Father has given me the seal of his approval."[67] The Messiah was sent by God to offer grace, forgiveness, and eternal life to people. And Jesus reminded us that "The thief comes only to steal and kill and destroy. I come that they may have life, and have it abundantly."[68] This is an opportunity to trust and to receive the Son of God and his abundant life.

---

64   John 15:15–16
65   Isaiah 42:6
66   1 Corinthians 13:7
67   John 6:27
68   John 10:10

Chapter 7:

Jesus, the Real Sacrificial Love

*For God so loved the world that he gave his only begotten
Son, that whosoever believed in him should not perish, but
have everlasting life.*

——John 3:16

The Cross

The message of the cross has been misunderstood by many. Why did a
Messiah, the Son of God, have to die on the cross? Why did he have
to be humiliated? What people don't know is that a sacrifice had to be
made; the blood had to be shared, and the price of deliverance for sinners
had to be paid for people to receive the grace of God and come back to
the right path. The Lamb of God had to be punished and crucified on the
cross as sacrifice to redeem people from their sins and heal their broken
hearts. Jesus said, "When you have lifted up the Son of Man on the cross,
then you will understand that I am He."[69] Jesus couldn't be the Messiah
without the cross.

The cross was part of God's hidden plan. Isaac, the son of Abraham,
took the wood and carried it to the place where God showed his father to
sacrifice him. The wood of Isaac was a symbol of the cross. There, Abraham
bound Isaac on top of the wood and laid him on the altar as sacrifice, but
Isaac couldn't die because he wasn't the Messiah, the promised Son of God.

---

69   John 8:28

Jesus is the Lamb of God who had to be bound and crucified to redeem people. He carried his cross to the place named Golgotha, where he was sacrificed as a burnt offering. Jesus said, "As Moses lifted up the serpent in the wilderness, even so must the son of man be lifted up, so anyone who believed in him should not perish but have eternal life."[70]People on Earth have been bitten and destroyed by the serpent (Devil) for a long time, and the Son of God had to be lifted up on the cross of Golgotha, so anyone who looks up at him will receive healing, forgiveness, blessing, and eternal life. The Devil did not understand the message hiding behind the cross. If he had, he wouldn't have been happy about the crucifixion of the Messiah. The apostle Paul wrote, "But the rulers of this world have not understood it. If they had, they would not have crucified our glorious Lord."[71] The prophecies prevent us that the Messiah will suffer and reject and those prophecies have been fulfilled by the crucifixion of Jesus Christ on the cross.

Jesus prepared his disciples for the crucifixion and said, "Listen, we're going up to Jerusalem, where all the predictions of the prophets concerning the Son of Man will come true. He will be handed over to the Romans, and he will be mocked, treated shamefully, and spit upon."[72] But when they took Jesus to crucify him on the cross and everything he said happened, the disciples were scared, frustrated, hurt, and powerless. They hid, and feared for their lives.

Jesus was crucified for telling the truth. He declared in public that he was the Son of God. Jesus asked his accusers "I have shown you many good works from the Father. For which of these are you going to stone me?"[73] The Jews answered, "It is not for a good work that we are going to stone you, but for blasphemy, because you, though only a human being, are making yourself God."[74] Jesus was accused of being the Messiah, the Son of God. The chief priest said, "According to our law, He must die, because He made Himself the son of God."[75] Jesus was the innocent Lamb of God, who gave his life as sacrifice to redeem sinners.

---

70 John 3:14–15
71 1 Corinthians 2:8
72 Luke 18:31–32
73 John 10:32
74 John 10:33
75 John 19:7

He was condemned and crucified because he said the truth about his own identity. Jesus said to Pilate, "You say I am a king. Actually, I was born and came into the world to testify to the truth. All who love the truth recognize that what I say is true."[76] One of criminals who were crucified with Jesus said this about him: "And we indeed have been condemned justly, for we are getting what we deserve for our deeds, but this man has done nothing wrong."[77] God used this criminal to proclaim Jesus's innocence and used the chief priest to accomplish and fulfill God's plan of Jesus dying on the cross.

Jesus was found guilty for being the Messiah, the innocent Son of the living God. He was accused of being truthful. His innocent blood had to sanctify and deliver God's people. Only through Jesus could God fulfill his salvation plan. Jesus was humiliated and punished to give us abundant life. Jesus said, "The father loves me because I sacrifice my life so I may take it back again. No one takes it from me, but I lay it down on my own. I have the right to lay it down, and I have the right to take it up again. I have received this command from My Father."[78] Jesus gave his life to give us eternal life. He had to die and share his blood on that cross to redeem humanity from its sins.

Jesus's death on the cross seems like a sad story with a bad ending. But those who understand God's salvation plan know that the death of Jesus on the cross is not a shameful story but a loving story with a good ending. We don't deserve the sacrifice of the innocent Son of God, but by love, grace, and compassion, he died for us. The cross is an amazing love story. Who else could give his life to save all the nations of the world? Only Jesus Christ voluntarily offered his life as sacrifice and was found holy and worthy enough to fulfill God's plan on the cross.

It is written, "For God loved the world in this way: He gave His One and only Son, so that everyone who believes in Him shall not perish but have eternal life."[79] The message of the cross is the message of love and grace. The cross is the only place where we could be delivered, healed, and forgiven. The price that Jesus had to pay for you and me was high. He

---

76 John 18:37
77 Luke 23:41
78 John 10:17–18
79 John 3:16

gave his own life in exchange for our liberty. Whoever needs healing and forgiveness has to look up to the cross of Jesus.

The cross means a lot for Christians because it is the place where every evil thing such as sin, doubt, faithlessness, sickness, poverty, and curses have been crucified and paid for. The cross brings freedom and blessing to people. There is not happiness on Earth without Jesus's sacrifice on the cross. The cross is the solution to man's weaknesses and failures. The Devil doesn't have power anymore over those who accept Jesus's sacrifice of love for them. We have to take Jesus's sacrifice on the cross as a loving gift and enjoy our liberty. It is written, "Therefore Jesus also suffered outside the city gate in order to sanctify the people by his own blood."[80]We are holy through Jesus's blood. We were forgiven on the cross and given the right to approach the throne of God through Jesus's blood. We can declare without any doubt that we are forgiven and holy. As holy people, we have the power to overcome the Devil. There is not condemnation for those who hide themselves under Jesus's blood. Jesus's sacrifice on the cross made evil and the flesh powerless. In Jesus we have the authority to overcome any weakness and any demonic power of darkness.

The cross of Jesus is the place of transference between our curses and Jesus's holiness. God's grace and blessing was given back there. On the cross we trade our old nature of sin and take on the new identity of holy children of God. The cross is the place where every Christian has to look and be transformed and delivered. Jesus took out our iniquities and our transgressions, and forgives our sin and gives us his holiness. In the cross every sickness and disease has been healed. Every guilty sentence has been paid for and forgiven. On the cross we are blessed and debt-free. John the Baptist declared this to the people: "Here is the Lamb of God who takes away the sin of the world!"[81]The cross offers to people an opportunity to become clean, innocent, and holy. On the cross, Jesus shared his blood as a new covenant between people and God. If you are reading this book and have never given your life to Jesus or recognized him as your Savior, this is your moment and time to confess Jesus as Lord and Savior of your life. Do it. Just say, "Lord Jesus; come into my heart and be my Lord and

---

80   Hebrews 13:12
81   John 1:29

my Savior. Forgive my sins; give me a new heart and make me a citizen of your kingdom. Amen."

This simple prayer will change everything in your life and your name will be written in the book of the Lamb of God. Find a good Bible and a good church and learn a new way of living with God. Jesus said in the gospel of John, "If you continue in my word, you really are my disciples. You will know the truth, and the truth will set you free."[82] Jesus is the only truth, and in him we are saved. Right now, rejoice in the Lord because Jesus made us citizens of the kingdom of God.

The Resurrection

The death of Jesus on the cross wasn't the end of his mission on Earth. Alive, Jesus fought for man's freedom, transformed people from the inside out, and showed God's power to people. He fought the darkness that surrounded God's people and prepared and brought light into their life. In Jesus people have the divine strength to overcome anything. But there was still a big enemy that Jesus had to fight and conquer, and that was death.

That enemy came into man's life through Adam and Eve's disobedience. Death is a consequence of disobedience. Jonah the prophet of God refused to follow God's instruction and found himself in the fish's belly between life and death. He prayed and cried to God, who after three days and three nights delivered him and brought him back to life. Jesus said, "This evil generation keeps asking me to show them a miraculous sign. But the only sign I will give them is the sign of Jonah."[83] The resurrection of Jesus was a sign that he truly was the Son of the living God. He died to bring life back to people who trust him. Empowered by God's Spirit, Jesus was resurrected and defeated death.

Jesus prophesied about his resurrection to his disciples, but when he died, they were sad and forgot what he and the scriptures had said about it. When someone we love passes away, we are sad and hurt because of the separation. Those disciples had built their lives around their master, Jesus. Without him they were lost, very hurt, and sad. But after three days and three nights, on the Sabbath, an angel of the Lord descended from heaven

---

82   John 8:31
83   Luke 11:29

and approached the tomb. He rolled back the stone and Jesus came back to life; he was resurrected. The tomb was empty.

The innocence of the Messiah won the battle of death and brought him back to life. Jesus had to come back to prove that he was the Messiah and the prince of life. He had to reassure people that he is the same yesterday, today, and forever. On resurrection day, the angel of God was the first to give the good news to the women who were there early in the morning. He said to them, "He is not here, for He has been resurrected, just as He said. Come and see the place where He lay."[84] The sadness of the women changed into joy about the good news of the resurrection, and they departed quickly from the tomb to announce it to others. The resurrection of Jesus is the good news of victory, hope, and joy. It means that death doesn't have power over Jesus and or over those who believe in him. In the book of John, Jesus said, "I am the resurrection and the life. Anyone who believes in me will live, even after dying, and everyone who lives and believe in me will never die."[85] Those in Jesus will have everlasting life. They don't have to go to eternal death in hell anymore.

The resurrection of Jesus is a powerful sign of God's mighty power and proof that God is a God of living creatures. People don't have to be scared about death anymore. The resurrection confirms for those who had some doubts that Jesus is the only way, truth, and life. The cross and the resurrection make Christianity unique, different, and powerful. Jesus died and was resurrected to give us eternal life with God. The resurrection of Jesus fulfills God's will of life for his people. It is a great victory against the Devil and his demons.

In the book of the prophet Isaiah it is written, "But those who die in the Lord will live; their bodies will rise again! Those who sleep in the earth will rise up and sing for joy."[86] We shall not be afraid of death because Jesus has power to rise up. Jesus said, "Now the ruler of this world will be cast out. As for me, if I am lifted up from earth, I will draw all people to myself."[87] Jesus with his death and his resurrection cast the Devil out and reestablished God's friendship with people on Earth.

---

84   Mark 16:6
85   John 11:25–26
86   Isaiah 26:19
87   John 12:31

When Jesus appeared after the resurrection to two of his disciples on their way to Emmaus, he was walking and talking with them, but they could not recognize him because they were under fear and deception. It was sad for Jesus to see his disciples defeated by fear and sadness. They were blinded and couldn't remember the scriptures. Jesus walked with them and reminded them what the scriptures said about him from Moses, the prophets, and the psalmist. He appeared to them to rebuild their confidence.

Jesus said to them, "When I was with you before, I told you that everything written about me in the Law of Moses and the prophets and in the Psalms must be fulfilled."[88] Jesus had to explain why it was necessary for him to die. Jesus said, "This is what is written: the Messiah would suffer and rise from the dead the third day and repentance for forgiveness of sins would be proclaimed in His name to all nations, beginning at Jerusalem. You are witness of these things."[89] He opened their spiritual eyes and gave them the understanding of the scriptures.

It is written in the letters to the Corinthians, "Then He appeared to more than five hundred brothers and sisters at one time, most of whom are still alive, through time, some have died. Then He appeared to James, then to all the apostles."[90] Those people were the witnesses to Jesus's resurrection. The resurrection brought back their confidence, the restoration, the spiritual healing, and the revival. The presence of Jesus brought light back to their lives and the assurance of a better future. Their anxieties, their deception, their fear, and their sadness disappeared because of the power of resurrection.

Jesus's disciples were ready for the great commission of being the witnesses to and successors of Jesus's inheritance. He said to them, "Peace to you! As the Father has sent Me, I also send you: Go into the world and preach the gospel to the whole creation"[91] and "It was also written that this message would be proclaimed in the authority of Messiah's name to all the nations."[92] Jesus sent his disciples to proclaim the good news of hope to all the nations in his name.

---

88   Luke 24:44
89   Luke 24:46
90   1 Corinthians 15:6–7
91   John 20:21
92   Luke 24:47

Jesus prayed for them and protected them and said, "Father, the hour has come. Glorify Your Son so that the Son may glorify You, for You gave Him authority over all flesh; so He may give eternal life to all You have given Him. This is eternal life: that they may know you, the only true God, and the One You have sent Jesus Christ. I have glorified you on the Earth by completing the work You gave me to do."[93] Jesus's work on Earth was amazing. In his hand the lost were saved. The blind gained sight. The sick were healed. The hungry were fed. The sinners were forgiven and the dead were raised. In the letter to the Hebrews it is written, "Jesus Christ is the same yesterday, and today and forever."[94] Jesus gave us power and tools to live a better life here on Earth and later the eternal life with himself and God. Jesus's mission shall continue and every knee shall bow down and proclaim that he is the Lord and Savior. In Jesus we are qualified to demonstrate God's power on Earth and proclaim freedom to captives and announce to all the nations that the years of God's favor and grace are among us through Jesus.

The Day of Pentecost

After the resurrection, the disciples were strong in faith and ready to accomplish Jesus's mission, but Jesus told them to not leave Jerusalem and wait for the Holy Spirit from heaven. Jesus said, "And now I will send the Holy Spirit, just as my Father promised. But stay here in the city until the Holy Spirit comes and fills you with power from heaven."[95] The Holy Spirit is the promised helper for people to continue Jesus's legacy on Earth.

Jesus said, "When the Spirit of truth comes, he will guide you into the truth. He will not speak on his own but will tell you what he has heard. He will tell you about the future."[96] The person of the Holy Spirit is very important; his job is to lead, to drive, and to give people directives from the Lord. Jesus said, "Anyone who speaks against the Son of Man can be forgiven, but anyone who blasphemes the Holy Spirit will not be forgiven."[97] The Holy Spirit faithfully empowers, guides, and helps people accomplish God's purpose for their life.

---

93   John 17:1–4
94   Hebrews 13:8
95   Luke 24:49
96   John 16:13
97   Luke 12:10

The disciples had to wait for the Holy Spirit before they started their ministries. When it was time for Jesus's departure to heaven, he said to them, "But you will receive power when the Holy Spirit comes upon you. And you will be my witnesses, telling people about me everywhere—in Jerusalem, throughout Judea, in Samaria, and to the ends of the Earth."[98] On Ascension Day, Jesus ascended into a cloud in heaven while the disciples were watching, until they could no longer see him; then the angels of God appeared among them and said, "Why are you standing here staring into heaven? Jesus has been taken from you into heaven, but someday He will return from heaven in the way you saw him go."[99] The disciples were amazed and filled with joy after watching the beautiful departure of the Messiah, the Son of the living God, to heaven. They believed that God was among them all the time, and together they were reunited in one place, praying and waiting for the Holy Spirit. On the day of Pentecost, the Holy Spirit came upon the disciples. It appeared like flames of fire, resting on each one of them. That day, they were filled with the Holy Spirit of God.

The Holy Spirit empowered them to speak different languages and gave them the ability for speech. It is written, "At that time the Spirit of the Lord will come powerfully upon you, and you will prophesy with them. You will be changed into a different person."[100] The Spirit of the Lord had come to empower them to prophesy and to become new people. The apostle Peter, excited and filled with power and courage, gave a wonderful sermon that day and became a leader of the group. Many nations were represented in Jerusalem; it was a time for festivities, and everyone could hear the magnificent acts of God in their own dialects and languages.

Jesus's disciples were ordinary men with no special training or special skill to understand or interpret the scriptures, but the power of God qualified them to do it. The power of the Holy Spirit changed their personalities, giving them authority, courage, and the ability to speak different languages and to preach the gospel to all the nations of the world. They were not scared and did not hide anymore.

They went everywhere to testify openly about Jesus and demonstrated God's power among people. On their first day of work, about three

---

98   Acts 1:8
99   Acts 1:11
100 1 Samuel 10:6

thousand people were added to them and were baptized in the name of Father, Son, and Holy Spirit. Every day the Lord added to their numbers more who were saved. After the day of Pentecost nothing could stop the disciples from spreading the good news of salvation around the world.

One day the apostles Peter and John healed a crippled beggar in Jesus's name. That news arrived to the authorities, and they decided to arrest them and put them in jail. The chief priest and religious teachers asked them, "By what power, or in whose name, have you done this?"[101] And then Peter, filled by the Holy Spirit, said to them, "Let me clearly state to all of you and to all the people of Israel that this man was healed by the powerful name of Jesus Christ the Nazarene, the man you crucified but whom God raised from dead."[102]No one could deny that they had performed miracles and signs in Jesus's name, and no one could stop them from telling everything they had seen and heard from Jesus and the Holy Spirit of God. The apostle Paul said, "For the kingdom of God is not just a lot of talk; it is living by God's power."[103] The disciples faithfully continued Jesus's mission on Earth.

Throughout this book we have talked about God the Father, Jesus the Son, and the Holy Spirit the Helper. Are they three different personalities or are they one? This question has divided many children of God. God is big and holy. This world can't contain him, and no one human creature can see his holy face and survive. He humiliated himself, becoming small and like one of us, coming down as Son to save us. He couldn't leave us alone and sent his Spirit to live inside us to change, empower, and help people overcome the darkness. We can't do anything without the Spirit of God. Jesus and the Holy Spirit are different representations and manifestations of the same God. The three entities are united, connecting and working together in harmony.

People are like God's broken cars. Jesus is like God's perfect mechanic. His job is to fix people, and the Holy Spirit is like gas that people need to move forward. Without gas, a car can't move. On the day of Pentecost, the Holy Spirit came upon the disciples like gas and empowered them to move. The Holy Spirit is the power from God. He gives people energy, strength,

---

101 Acts 4:7
102 Acts 4:10
103 1 Corinthians 4:20

and courage. The Holy Spirit works only in the people fixed by Jesus. He continues the job started by Jesus. Without the Holy Spirit people can't serve God. It does not matter what background people come from, Jesus can fix them, and the Holy Spirit will give them light and empower them to serve in the kingdom of God. Anyone with the desire to serve the Lord is qualified to work for him.

The only thing required from people is to say yes to God's will, to trust him, and to surrender their life to God and pay attention to the command of the Holy Spirit. People can't serve God without his power. Obedience is the key to success with God. Most of the time people make the mistake of trying to command the Holy Spirit. It is like a blind person driving a person who can see and who knows the direction. That does not make sense at all, but it's what people do when they are doing what they want and not following the Holy Spirit's instructions. God knew people needed help, and he sent his Holy Spirit to be their eyes and guide them in the light.

There are many false prophets with false spirits who are driving God's people on the darkest roads of death. They are saying and doing what people want to hear. Don't give yourself to them. People have to search for God on their own and trust the voice of God inside them. In everything, people have to request God's opinion and approval before proceeding, and God will guide and direct their paths. Only the Holy Spirit of the Lord is able to show us the true way and the true light.

We have learned a lot about the trinity of Father, Son, and Holy Spirit. We know that Jesus is the only way, the only truth, and the life. He is not a stranger to us anymore, and his name is our treasure. He said in the gospel of John, "Until now you have asked for nothing in my name. But from now everything you ask in my name, you shall receive because I want you to have abundant joy."[104] Jesus wants us to enjoy abundant life, to have his peace, and to ask for anything we need and want from God in his name. The Holy Spirit is upon us to anoint us for good work.

The grace of God is available for those who repent with a sincere heart. God never gives up on anyone who has his breath. As soon as people repent and cry for God's help, the grace of God comes upon them and gives them power to overcome anything. God is faithful and keeps his promise even when people are faithless. God still protects the godly and the ungodly,

---

104 John 16:24, 26–27

giving them the same opportunities. But the day will come when God separates the godly from the ungodly. They will be judged for not receiving his salvation and for taking God's presence for granted and not thanking him for all he has done for them.

There is still time to repent and come back to God. God will forgive and welcome anyone into his kingdom. It is written in the letter to the Romans, "Blessed are those whose iniquities are forgiven and whose sins are covered."[105] Jesus said in the parable of the lost sheep, "There is more joy in heaven over one lost sinner who repents and returns to God than over ninety-nine others who are righteous and haven't strayed away."[106] When a sheep is lost, the shepherd has to leave everything and go search for it until he finds it. And when he finds it, he will joyfully carry it home on his shoulders. There is more joy in heaven when the lost children of God are found and return to him. That is God's love, full of grace and patience.

If we are still alive, it is because God is giving time and opportunity for people all around the world to repent and to become who he has called them to be, the children of light. Without Jesus, we can't get out of addictions, troubles, or any kind of struggles. Jesus never hesitates to share a table with sinners and the lost. He said, "For the Son of Man came to seek and save those are lost."[107] He came to find those who are lost and going straight to hell, and to change their course, showing them the way to return home and giving them a chance to enter the kingdom of God.

Jesus didn't share his blood of covenant for nothing, but to give real life, to save and to heal sinners. He took their curses and gave them blessing. He brings mercy, hope, grace, and forgiveness to those who really need it. One day, standing in the temple, Jesus read this scripture of the prophet Isaiah: "The Spirit of the Lord is upon me, for He has anointed me to bring good news to the poor. He has sent me to proclaim that captives will be released, that the blind will see, that the oppressed will be set free, and that the time of the Lord's favor has come."[108] This is a time of God's favor; people are set free to enjoy life. God said through his prophet, "He will give justice to the poor and make fair decisions for the exploited."[109]

---

105 Romans 4:7
106 Luke 15:7
107 Luke 19:10
108 Isaiah 61:1–2
109 Isaiah 11:4

There is hope in Jesus. He didn't come to judge people for what they had done, but to give people the chance to change and be transformed by his power. In him people have opportunities, liberty, peace, joy, and eternal life.

Jesus is calling to everyone, "Come to me, all of you who are weary and carry heavy burdens, and I will give you rest."[110] Jesus is able to fix anyone and everything. He is able to take everyone's burdens and turn them into blessings. He came from heaven with the purpose of delivering people from the heaviness of sins; to help them make wise and right choices; and to empower them to do well and make their life light, simple, and enjoyable like in heaven.

---

110 Matthew 11:28

Chapter 8:

The Foundations of a Successful Spiritual Life

Trust in the Lord and do good works. Then you will live safely in the Land and prosper. Take delight in the Lord, and he will give you your heart's desires.

——Psalm 37:3—4

No one can teach people how to live a successful spiritual life like Jesus. He is the greatest teacher of all time, with supernatural wisdom. People called him Rabbi (which translated means "Teacher") because of his incredible knowledge and wisdom. Jesus brought to the Earth unknown revelations and a new way of understanding and living with the heavenly Father. Jesus said, "Let me teach you, because I am humble and gentle at heart, and will find rest for your souls. For my yoke is easy to bear, and the burden I give you is light,"[111] Jesus simplified things and made it easier for people to learn and get close to God.

Jesus's life itself was a teaching of how to handle earthly life and stay faithful to God. He explained the scriptures with passion, authority, and confidence. A man named Nicodemus, inspired by the Holy Spirit, said to Jesus, "Rabbi, we know that you come from God as a Teacher, for no one could perform these signs you do unless God were with him."[112] Jesus was a great teacher from God. As a good teacher, Jesus had disciples and multitudes following him every day to hear and learn heavenly lessons. Jesus said, "For I have come down from heaven to do the will of God who

111 Matthew 11:29
112 John 3:2

sent me, not to do my own will."[113] God's will is for everyone to know the truth and be set free from the Devil's slavery.

Jesus said, "Anyone who listens to my teaching and practices it, is wise like a person who builds a house on solid rock. Though the rain comes in torrents and the floodwaters rise and the winds beat against that house, it won't collapse because it is built on bedrock."[114] Jesus is the solid rock on which we have to build our spiritual life. Nothing can shake those who sincerely make Jesus their rock and practice his teaching. The apostle Paul wrote in the letter to Timothy, "All Scriptures are inspired by God and useful to teach us what is wrong in our lives. It corrects us when we are wrong and teaches us to do what is right."[115] Jesus's teachings are wonderful and are for people who thirst for peace, knowledge, and wisdom. When we know better, we do better and right. To build a successful spiritual life we need the word of God, patience, and perseverance. It has to be a personal initiative and a goal to pursue with love and passion. It needs humility and trust because it is a progressive process. The more we know, the more we progress and grow spiritually. It is a course to pursue with persistence, and at the end there will be a prize for the winner. The apostle Paul said, "I press on to reach the end of the race and receive the heavenly prize for which God, through Christ Jesus, is calling us."[116] There are basic steps that can help people start a strong spiritual connection with God and have a solid foundation in Christian faith. Those basic steps are as follows:

- Know God Almighty.
- Discover and claim a new identity in Jesus Christ.
- Repent and be humble.
- Have faith and maintain a holy life of prayer.
- Do not be anxious and do not worry.

Know God Almighty

Those who want to grow spiritually have to acknowledge that there is a most high power reigning, controlling, and taking care of everything.

---

113 John 6:38
114 Matthew 7:24–25
115 2 Timothy 3:16
116 Philippians 3:14

God said, "You have been chosen to know me, believe me, and understand that I alone am God. There is no other God; there never has been, and there never will be."[117] There is no way that people could exist without God. He is Almighty, he is the Most High, and his name is Yahweh, the God of the Holy Bible. Acknowledging his presence is a first step toward discovering the truth. People have to know him and his value to love him and to love themselves. He is open to people who approach him and want to know him better.

But to have intimacy with him takes personal effort and is an individual decision. That intimacy comes with the knowledge of who he is. For that, reading, meditating on, and understanding the word of God are the most important steps to take when we search to know the Most High God. Only those people who trust him, persevere, and persist in learning and staying in his way will be rewarded and see him face to face one day. God said to Joshua, "This book of instruction must not depart from your mouth; meditate on it day and night; for then you will prosper and succeed in whatever you do."[118] There is nowhere else people can start to learn about and know God except the Bible. God by his Spirit inspired people to write the Bible, and in it, he talks about and opens himself to anyone who wants to be close to him. God always wants people to know him very well and to discover his identity and his love for them. Many people have tried to find God but in the wrong place. The Bible is a record of God's words and wisdom; it presents God and his prescriptions. In the Bible is everything people need to have a happy life of peace and prosperity.

The reading of and the meditation on the Bible gives wisdom, knowledge, prosperity, and success that no one can take away. God blessed many people in the Bible because they were intimate with him. Their success comes from knowing and obeying God. It is written in the book of Hosea, "Oh, that we might know the Lord! Let us press on to know Him. He will respond to us surely as the arrival of dawn or the coming of rains in early spring."[119] People have to press on to know God first, and everything shall be given to them.

---

117 Isaiah 43:10b–c
118 Joshua 1:8
119 Hosea 6:3

Through the reading of the scripture we discover God's different personalities and characteristics. We know that God has eyes, ears, a mouth, and a heart like us. But as a creator of everything God is immense and huge and can't be described. In the book of Isaiah, God said, "Heaven is my throne, and the Earth is my footstool. Could you build me such a resting place? My hands have made both heaven and Earth; they and everything in them are mine. I the Lord have spoken."[120] If heaven is God's throne and the Earth is his footstool, its means both heaven and earth are under God's sovereignty and nothing that they contain can be considerate like god.

God is above everything that he made by his hands. Everything that exists was created by God in seven days. When God gave the Ten Commandments to Moses, he said, "You must not make for yourself an idol of any kind, or an image of anything in the heaven or on the Earth or in the sea."[121] We shall not have any other gods because they are false and powerless. There is just one God. He is Alpha and Omega, omnipresent, omniscient, almighty, and sovereign. He is holy and lives in the most high place where he is able to hear, to see, and to answer the prayers of all the people of the planet at the same time.

His power sustains both heaven and Earth so that they do not fall apart. Because of his power and love we live and exist. King David said to God, "For you are great and perform wonderful deeds. You alone are God."[122] Everything that exists has to have a creator. Who claims to be the creator of the sky, the sea, the moon, and the sun? Who orders the seasons to change? Who made people white, black, or yellow? Who develops an embryo in a woman's womb? Who takes care of and protects the animals and trees of the jungle? The answer is found in the Bible, where God claims to be the creator and the protector of everything.

All the people of the world shall be proud and honor God for who he is and for what he has done and is doing for them. When we know God, we discover how powerless we are and how powerful he is. We are nothing without his Spirit. One of the religious teachers asked Jesus, "Of all the commandments, which is the most important?" and Jesus answered, "The

---

120 Isaiah 66:1–2
121 Deuteronomy 5:8
122 Psalm 86:10

most important commandment is this; you must love the Lord your God with all your heart, with all your soul, with all your mind, and with all your strength."[123] When we know God, is impossible to not love him with all our heart, soul, and mind.

Loving God also means obeying his commands and following his instructions. It is easy to obey God when we love him with all our heart. Jesus said, "There is no greater love than to lay down one's life for one's friends."[124] God loved us first and gave his son's life for us. Knowing that God Almighty, with all his power and majesty, loves us and takes care of us gives us strength and the ability to break any barriers. It also makes life more exciting.

Christianity brought back intimacy between God and people. Through Jesus, God bends down to touch, heal, and revive his people. Jesus encourages people to approach God and to call him Father. We are all invited by Jesus to be God's friend. Being God's friend is a privilege and an honor. Jesus said, "Now you are my friends, since I have told you everything the Father told me."[125]In Jesus we see and know the Father. And he said, "Just believe that I am in the Father and the Father is in me."[126] We have to trust Jesus and his words and learn from him how to be close and intimate with God. God said, "From eternity to eternity I am God. No one can snatch anyone out of my hand. No one can undo what I have done."[127] In Jesus we will live the eternity of God, and no one can snatch us from his mighty hand.

I learn through the scriptures that God is an unseen presence, unshakeable, unchangeable, unstoppable, immeasurable, big, holy, love, goodness, faithful, a provider, a miracle maker, infinite power, and an excellent Father. We have to approach him and he will reveal himself. Knowing him, loving and obeying him, and making peace with him are the keys to succeeding in everything and to having rest for eternity.

Discover and Claim a New Identity in Jesus Christ

---

123 Matthew 22:37
124 John 15:13
125 John 15:15b
126 John 14:11
127 Isaiah 43:13

Without Jesus, people were living in the flesh under condemnation, guilt, shame, and curse. It is written, "You were dead through the trespasses and sins, in which you once lived, following the course of this world, following the ruler of the power of the air, the spirit that is now at work among those who are disobedient."[128] But God, who is rich in mercy, made us alive together under Jesus's covenant. With Jesus, people live under grace, peace, freedom, and blessing. It is written again, "For by grace you have been saved through faith, and this not your own doing; it is the gift of God."[129] Many people have received Jesus by faith and don't claim their gift and their right as children of the Most High God. It is written, "But to all who received him, who believed in His name, He gave power to become children of God."[130] People are protected and have power when they become Christians, but most of the time they don't use it or they ignore the fact that they have it. The story of a lost baby eagle can illustrate how hard and frustrating it is for someone to not remember his identity and be lost in a strange land.

One day an eagle's mother leaves her new little eagle in the nest and goes out to search for food to feed him. After her departure, the curious baby eagle moves out of his nest even though he does not know how to fly yet. By accident, the baby eagle falls down to the ground and there is no one to rescue him. He cries and looks for his mother, but she doesn't appear.

Later the baby eagle sees a family of birds walking on the ground. He says to himself, "Finally the rescue has come," and he tries to copy the way they are walking and follows them. It is a chicken family searching for food on the ground. When Mother Chicken sees the little eagle coming toward them, she begins to run and hide her little chicks. The innocent little eagle doesn't understand why they are running away from him. He thinks maybe they are teaching him how to walk and decides to continue to run after them.

Then after a while, Mother Chicken realizes that something is wrong with the little baby eagle. "Maybe he is lost," she says to herself. She stops running and the baby eagle joins them. As he approaches them, Mother

---

128 Ephesians 2:1–2
129 Ephesians 2:8
130 John 1:12

Chicken begins to peck him with her beak and treat him badly. The little eagle cries and suffers, but he doesn't know what to do or where to go. He doesn't even understand why Mother Chicken is punishing and attacking him. Finally Mother Chicken gets tired and lets the lost baby eagle follow them.

Later, the little eagle completely copies the chickens' lifestyle, but he isn't perfect. The chickens always mock him, laugh at him, and make jokes about how he looks. They call him a big, ugly, fat bird. He does not look like them or walk exactly like them, and he does not speak their language well. It is very frustrating and sad for the baby eagle, and he begins to question himself: "Why don't they like me? What did I do? Why do I look different? Where did I come from? Why don't I speak and walk like them?" And he decides to challenge himself to improve and become the best chicken ever. He thinks it is the only way they will stop mocking him and hating him.

Meanwhile, the eagle's mother is sad about losing her baby and searches for him everywhere, every day. She never stops believing that her son is alive and that one day she will find him. One day she is hunting, and from far up in the sky, she sees the chicken family and decides to attack them and take one of them. As she approaches and is ready to pick one, she notices that one of the chickens looks different. He is big and has a different appearance. She backs up and hides on a tree's branches and carefully observes the strange chicken.

Immediately she knows that the big chicken is her lost son, living like a chicken. She is happy to have found her son but also very sad to see how her son is humiliated and living like a chicken. She says to herself, "I cannot leave him there; I have to rescue him and teach him to live like an eagle." Every day Mother Eagle follows the chicken family, searching for a way to rescue and reconnect with her son. Mother Eagle decides to just speak the eagle language, hoping that her son will understand her with time.

The little eagle begins to hear a noise sounding like it is coming from up high. He asks the chickens if they hear the same voice, but they laugh at him, calling him crazy. Only he can hear it. But Mother Eagle is determined to save her son and take him away from the chickens. Other eagles are mad and upset with Mother Eagle because of her determination.

They don't understand why she spends her time and energy trying to rescue her loser son who lives like a chicken.

The other eagles want to hunt those chickens, but Mother Eagle spends her days and nights protecting them because of her son. She does not let them approach or attack them. With time, Mother Eagle's noise begins to make sense to her son's ears and he begins to decode words, and finally one day he understands completely the eagle's language and understands what the voice is saying. He learns that he isn't a chicken; he is an eagle, and only he can hear that language. Then the little eagle decides to trust the voice of the strange creature that is talking to him. He looks up in the sky and sees his mother flying beautifully in the air.

For the first time Mother Eagle sees her son put his head up, and she understands that he has been listening to her. She is happy and reveals his eagle identity to him. The little eagle is amazed to learn that he can fly like that big bird that looks exactly like him. The little eagle discovers the mystery of his weakness and learns to fly. A few days later he flies and goes back into the sky where he belongs, and lives happily forever.

God's people are like eagles living in the chickens' world. They are suffering at the hands of chickens because they don't know who they are. They are trying to satisfy the chickens' world, spending energy and time with a wrong identity and learning wrong ideologies. Living in the wrong environment and with the wrong people is painful. Their rejection and their wrong judgment create frustrations and suffering for people who don't know they are in the wrong place and with the wrong people. That is a root of pain, suffering, and suicide for most of the people who don't know their true value.

The true value of a human being is the Spirit of God inside them. Without it, humans are like animals. The Devil attacks those who are special and have the Spirit of God working inside them. Jesus said, "The world would love you as one of its own if you belonged to it, but you are no longer part of world. I chose you to come out of the world, so it hates you."[131] Sometimes, the world knows who we are and we don't. It hates us for being chosen by God. Most of the criticism and suffering that God's people experience is caused by their identity as children of God. When you

---

131 John 15:19

didn't do anything wrong and people hate you, don't worry; praise God and thank him for choosing you and separating you from the world.

This world is still protected by God because of his people who live in it. But when all of them hear the good news of salvation and learn to fly, they will be taken into heaven, and then this world will be destroyed. Because of who they are in Jesus, this world hates them. But if God's people discover their power and learn how to use it, they will enjoy their lives more and will change their surroundings. In Jesus, people are protected and have the strength to defeat this world and its ugly face. If we know our identity in Jesus, we will no longer suffer.

The crisis of identity brings conflicts, confusion, and frustration in people's personalities, and it is very painful. The desperate little eagle in the story was praying and asking to become the best chicken he could. Many people with a crisis of identity pray and ask God to make them someone they are not created to be. But God can't help people become who they are not. People have to ask God to make them the best in what they were destined to become.

Life is the best investment people have. Without life we can't do anything. We have to value that life by doing right and by becoming our better selves. People have to believe that God knows best and trust him for making them who they are. The little eagle is the perfect example to help people discover their identity in Christ Jesus. When people receive Jesus into their lives, they have to let him change their old sinful natures and give them new identities as children of God.

Many people accept Jesus but don't let him change them from the inside out. It's like living in the sky not wanting to fly and continuing to walk. That doesn't make sense, because creatures of the sky fly and those on the ground walk. When you are living in the sky, you have to fly. In Jesus, people have to have a new way of thinking and living. The old person has to die and the new person has to live. A person who decides to follow Jesus has to be prepared to live a new life like God's child. The little eagle without training and without his mother by his side tried to fly, but he fell to the ground in the hands of enemy chickens because he wasn't prepared to fly yet. It is impossible to succeed alone in God's ways. We need each other's hands to continue in Jesus's will.

The prophet Isaiah said, "But those who trust in the Lord will find new strength. They will soar high on wings like eagles. They will run and not grow weary. They will walk and not faint."[132] Christians are like eagles: they have to run and not grow weary. God renews their strength every morning for them to walk in the victory. True children of God have to trust and persevere in God's promises. In the letter to the Ephesians, the apostle Paul said, "And now you Gentiles have also heard the truth, the good news that God saves you. And when you believed in Christ, He identified you as his own."[133]When Jesus identifies people as his own, he gives them his mind and name as their treasure to use on Earth. In his name people run and do not stop and they walk and do not faint. In Jesus people have strength and power to overcome anything. Jesus said in the book of Luke, "Blessed are all who heard the word of God and put it into practice."[134] Christianity is a lifestyle; enjoy it, practice it, and live it. The Christian life is exciting when we are truly giving our hearts to Jesus. If we know Jesus's voice and obey his commands, we will experience supernatural miracles. As believers, we have to claim our right as children of the Most High. We have to live under the new identity given by Jesus.

In Jesus people are born again and are new creatures. It is written, "We're born, not of blood or of the will of the flesh or the will of man, but of God."[135] Our past is forgotten, and in Jesus we are renewed and ready to experience happiness and a peaceful life. It is written in the letter to the Ephesians, "Throw off your old sinful nature and your former way of life, which is corrupted by lust and deception. Instead let the Spirit renew your thoughts and attitudes. Put on your new nature, created to be like God; truly righteous and holy."[136]God's job is to help people become who he created them to be, truly righteous and holy. People have to avoid wasting time and energy trying to become someone they are not. They will never find peace or joy outside God's will for their life. Learn to thank God for who he is and for who he made us: "an act of love and faithfulness." God doesn't ever make mistakes; he made us to glorify his name. Knowing

---

132 Isaiah 40:31
133 Ephesians 1:13
134 Luke 11:28
135 John 1:13
136 Ephesians 4:22–24

our identity and accepting it as a gift from God with joy and gratitude is another key to happiness.

Repent and Be Humble

Repentance happens when people or nations feel sorrow or regret about something they have done wrong or left undone either through ignorance or on purpose. With sincere and open hearts, the people or nations come before God to ask for forgiveness. When people recognize that they have sinned and promise to turn away from them, God always forgives and forgets. God spoke through the prophet Ezekiel and said, "Repent and turn away from your sins. Don't let them destroy you. Put all your rebellion behind you, and find yourselves a new heart and a new spirit. For why should you die O people of Israel? I don't want you to die, says the Sovereign Lord. Turn back and live!"[137] It is not God who destroys people but their rebellion. Repentance is a door opened by God to save and protect people from death. People always make wrong choices and commit mistakes. God, who is love, is always ready to forgive those who repent and come back to him. Repentance brings God's grace and mercy to people. Grace and mercy are available for all people ready to put their rebellion behind them. Jesus said, "No, I tell you again that unless you repent, you will perish, too."[138] Through Jesus's blood every sin will be forgiven and wiped away.

Only humble people have the courage to recognize that they were wrong and want to change and need Jesus's help. Humility reminds people that they are nothing and God is everything. God is the perfect example of humility. He has power, but he comes down and works in silence for people and never shows up to give himself glory. Jesus has everything in heaven, but he gave his life to help people and save them. He suffered and was humiliated, but he didn't complain. He humbled himself by dying on the cross like a criminal.

Today we don't have many humble leaders who can give their life for others like Jesus did. In Isaiah, God said, "I look favorably on this kind of person: one who is humble, submissive in spirit, and who trembles at

---

137 Ezekiel 18:30–32
138 Luke 13:5

my word."[139] Being humble is another requirement of pleasing God. Jesus said, "So anyone who becomes as humble as this child is the greatest in the kingdom of heaven."[140] People's idea of what makes a great man is different from God's. For people, a great man is a man who is wealthy, has a lot of money, possessions, and influence, and doesn't have to be humble. Humbleness is like a weakness to be avoided. A great man has to be served and has to have first place everywhere. But for God, a great man can have wealth, influence, and money but humbles himself and loves to serve and put others first.

Jesus said in the gospel of Matthew, "But many who are the greatest now will be least important then, and those who seem least important now will be the great then."[141] Humble people know that in Jesus they are branches and he is the vine. He commands and they obey without complaining or murmuring. Jesus said to his disciples, "But among you it will be different. Whoever wants to be a leader among you must be a servant, and whoever wants to be first among you must be the slave of everyone else, for even the Son of Man came not to be served but to serve others."[142]God chooses people to serve and to lead by example. Whoever exalts himself will be humbled, and the most humble will be elevated by God. Serving and helping others is Jesus's commandment. Around us are people in need and alone who are craving and crying for help and support. Jesus showed compassion and mercy for them. We have to show God's love to others by giving them hope and extending our hands to help. How can we be sure that we love a God we don't see if we don't love those who are living among us? We have to prove that God's love is real by being active and present to people in need. That's how people will believe in love, compassion, and mercy once again.

Homeless and poor people all around the world need to hear the good news of hope and learn God's way of living. God uses his people to help other people. God blesses people to be a blessing to others. Jesus said, "When you give a lunch or a dinner; don't invite your friends, your brothers, your relatives, or your rich neighbors; for they will invite you

---

139 Isaiah 66:2
140 Matthew 18:4
141 Matthew 19:30
142 Mark 10:43–45

back, and that will be your only reward. Instead, invite those who are poor, maimed, lame, or blind. Then at the resurrection of righteous, God will reward you for inviting those who could not repay you."[143] All gifts, talents, positions, and promotions that we receive from God have to be used for his glory. God's light can't be hidden; it has to shine to advance God's kingdom. The apostle James wrote, "Humble yourselves before the Lord, and He will lift you up in honor."[144] The humblest people will be rewarded, honored, blessed, and elevated by God.

Have Faith and Maintain a Holy Life of Prayer

Faith comes and grows by hearing the word of God. In Romans, it is written, "We are made right with God by placing our faith in Jesus Christ. And this is true for everyone who believes, no matter who we are."[145] Jesus is the word of God in flesh. It is written, "In the beginning was the word, and the word was with God and the word was God."[146] Everything began by the word and faith was born through the word. Then it is written that "He was in the beginning with God. All things come into being through him, and without him not one thing came into being."[147] In him we learn and live.

In Hebrews it is also written, "And my righteous ones will live by faith. But I will take no pleasure in anyone who turns away."[148] Living by faith means living through Jesus; believing and trusting him. What we believe and trust comes from what we have heard and learned. People are what they believe. If people live in a cruel environment and are exposed to cruel education, they will become cruel and believe that they are right. Their absolute truth is a life of crime.

It's hard for people to convince others that their truth is not the absolute truth. But Jesus by his power and charisma was able to prove to people that God is the absolute truth through the evidence of the miraculous works he has done. Jesus said, "But if I do his work, believes in the evidence of the miraculous works I have done, even if you don't believe me. Then you will

---

143 Luke 14:12
144 James 4:10
145 Romans 3:22
146 John 1:1
147 John 1:2–3
148 Hebrews 10:38

know and understand that the Father is in me and I am in the Father."[149] By hearing, learning, and practicing Jesus's words, people's faith grows and miracles happen.

No matter what people believe, they always expect some result at the end. If you don't know what you believe, look at your present life. Where are you? And what is your state of mind like? Are you satisfied? If not, please give Jesus a chance to help you. Who we are today is the result of what we believed yesterday. Faith in Jesus produces fruit and changes people's lives. What people believe by faith today will come to pass in the future. In the book of Proverbs it is written, "Trust in the Lord with all your heart; do not depend on your own understanding. Seek his will in all you do, and he will show you which path to take."[150] There is power in faith.

It written that "Faith is the assurance of things hoped for, the conviction of things not seen."[151] Faith brings the unseen into existence; the untouchable becomes touchable. Faith is a requirement to please God and see his manifestation. King David said to God, "I will call you wherever I'm in trouble, and you will answer me."[152] He was sure that God would answer him and deliver him from his troubles. By faith, people trust God's words and do whatever God asks them to do, even when they don't understand. In the letter to the Hebrews it is written, "Faith is the confidence that what we hope for will actually happen; it gives us assurance about things we cannot see."[153]Abraham believed God by faith and God counted him as righteous. The prophet Daniel trusted God and didn't deny him even if he had to lose his life. Daniel had faith in God's promises. King David had faith and respect for God's anointment. He waited with patience for his time to become a king. God always rewards those who live by faith. In the letter to the Hebrews, Paul said, "It is impossible to please God without faith. Anyone who wants to come to Him must believe that God exists and he rewards those who sincerely seek him."[154] People are counted as righteous and rewarded by God because of their faith in God's words.

---

149 John 10:38
150 Proverbs 3:5–6
151 Hebrews 11:1
152 Psalm 86:7
153 Hebrews 11:1
154 Hebrews 11:6

Faith is the ability to believe without any doubt that what God said is truth and that it will happen. People with great faith are like "trees planted along the riverbank, bearing fruit each season. Their leaves never wither, and they prosper in all they do."[155] Faith brings hope, happiness, and blessing. In the gospel of John, Jesus said, "I tell you the truth, anyone who had faith in me will do what I have done. He will do even greater things than these."[156] Faith is the key that opens the door of supernatural blessing. Faith has the power to solve the impossible. There are two secrets that make faith work:

- Staying connected to the author and the finisher of the faith. Jesus said, "Yes, I am the vine, you are the branches. Those who remain in me, and I in them, will produce much fruit. For apart from me you can do nothing."[157]

- Believing without doubt. Jesus said, "I assure you: if anyone says to this mountain, be lifted up and thrown into the sea, and does not doubt in his heart, but believes that what he says will happen, it will be done for him."[158]

Faithful people use prayer to connect with God. Prayer is their communication with God. People express their feelings to God through prayer. God lets people freely talk to him. In prayer people can talk, cry, and even laugh with God. Where there is trust, there is also liberty to speak. By praying, people believe that God is listening and that he will surely answer their requests. Jesus said in the gospel of Mark, "I tell you, you can pray for anything and if you believe that you've received, it will be yours."[159] Prayer brings people close to God and creates intimacy and friendship between God and people.

The only way to be in touch with God is in prayer, in praise, and in meditation. People have to learn to spend time with their creator. Prayer is a powerful spiritual tool. It touches God's heart and brings his presence among people. The apostle Paul wrote, "I urge you, first of all, to pray for all people. Ask God to help them, intercede on their behalf, and give

---

155 Psalm 1:3
156 John 14:12
157 John 15:5
158 Mark 11:22
159 Mark 11:24

thanks for them."[160] God hears prayers and understands man's expressions of the heart. People of every tongue and language can pray and God will hear them. People can ask anything of God in prayer, and God, who knows and has everything, will respond.

Jesus reminded his disciples that they needed to pray to not be tempted. He said, "Get up and pray, so that you will not give in to temptation."[161] Prayer is the greatest tool to use to see God's manifestation. It reminds people that God is holy and that only holy people can approach him. We can use prayer in any circumstance and can even avoid calamity and disaster by the power of prayer. Jesus's disciples continuously prayed. It is written in the book of Acts, "When they heard the report, all the believers lifted their voices together in prayer to God."[162] Prayer has to be something private between God and the one who is praying. Jesus taught his disciples how to pray and said, "Whenever you pray, you must not be like the hypocrites, because they love to pray standing in the synagogues and the street corners to be seen by people … But when you pray, go into your private room, shut your door, and pray to your Father who is in secret. And your Father who sees in secret will reward you."[163] We don't have to stand in public with the intention of getting people's attention and begin to pray for everyone to hear. Prayer can be silent or loud, but it is for God's attention only and without hypocrisy.

People pray to God because they need God and love him. People sing, worship, and praise God because he is wonderful and powerful. He loves them and answers their prayer requests. The prophet Isaiah said, "Sing to the Lord, for he has done wonderful things. Make known His praise around the world."[164] Where love is, there is admiration, compliment, joy, and faithfulness. Any relationship without love, trust, and good communication can't survive. To have intimacy with God, people have to have these three virtues: love, trust, and prayer. A good prayer always arrives before God's throne and always receives his agreement. It is written, "The prayer of the righteous person is powerful and effective."[165]

---

160 1 Timothy 2:1
161 Luke 22: 46b
162 Acts 4:24
163 Matthew 6:5–6
164 Isaiah 12:5
165 James 5:16b

Do Not Be Anxious and Do Not Worry

This world is full of people with ugly hearts operating under the Devil's influence. They hate justice and love to hurt others. But they have been defeated by the power of the blood of Jesus Christ. The prophets of God and Jesus suffered in their hands, but at the end God gave them victory over their enemies.

The prophet Elijah was a wonderful man of God. He showed God's power among people and did what was right in God's eyes. But one day a queen named Jezebel sent this message to him: "May the gods strike me and even kill me if by this time tomorrow I have not killed you."[166] When the prophet heard that message, he was afraid and fled for his life. He went on alone into the wilderness. But God came to his rescue and empowered him, and at the end of his mission on Earth, he was taken into heaven and didn't die.

When he was about to be arrested, Jesus said to his disciples, "My soul is crushed with grief to the point of death. Stay here and keep watch with me."[167] He was arrested, humiliated, and died on the cross like a criminal, but by the power of God he was resurrected and went in glory back to heaven.

Sometimes even the greatest men of God feel sad when the world hates them and when they have to pass through tribulations and suffering, but they never stop serving God or give up on their mission or lose their mind. Jesus said, "The world hates them because they do not belong to the world, just as I do not belong to the world."[168] The prophets and the disciples of Jesus didn't give up on God because of trials and haters. In their weakness, they cried to God for help and he was always by their side to give them strength, comfort, and courage.

Jesus at his breaking point cried to God and said, "My Father! If it is possible, let this cup of suffering be taken from me. Yet I want your will to be done, not mine."[169] Jesus knew that God's will had to be done, and even it was hard and the pain was unbearable, he did not give up. He was determined to finish his mission on Earth. His life is a lesson for our life.

---

166 1 Kings 19:2
167 Matthew 26; 38
168 John 17:14
169 Matthew 26:39

If he suffered and didn't give up, that means we can't give up even when we pass by tribulations or tough time. We have to cry to the Lord for help. The prophet Elijah at his breaking point ran to God's Mountain and God took care of him.

People have to remember God's love in any situation and run to him in time of trouble and suffering. He is our father and knows how we feel, and with him on our side, we will win any challenge. The love we have for God makes us strong to endure and to persevere through trials and suffering. It is written, "Can anything ever separate us from Christ's love? Does it mean He no longer loves us if we have trouble or calamity, or are persecuted, or hungry, or destitute, or in danger, or threatened with death?"[170] Being in trouble or in pain doesn't mean we are defeated. Our reaction to the circumstances good or bad determines if we will win or lose. If we're scared, that means we will lose, and if we remain confident and trust God, that means we will win.

Our faith is faith when it is being tested, and when we exercise it, it grows. If we trust God and have confidence in his words, we will always have victory. But if we are scared and worried, it means we are giving power to the enemy who wants us to fail. Only in God's hands can we have the strength to overcome fear and worries. Fear and worries are the enemies of trust and faith. In Joshua, God said to him, "Haven't I commanded you: be strong and courageous? Do not be afraid or discouraged, for the Lord your God is with you wherever you go."[171] The challenges in life are just tests of faith. We don't have to be afraid of this world and its challenges. We have to be determined to face them and continuously focus on God's promises. We are not alone; the Spirit of God is with us to help and to empower us to win. God said, "Don't be afraid, for I am with you. Don't de discouraged, for I am your God. I will strengthen you and help you. I will hold you up with my victorious right hand."[172] Yes, God is keeping us safe from the ugliness of this world. We have to seek God's presence and trust him because he promises that his victorious right hand will fight for us every day.

---

170 Romans 8:35
171 Joshua 1:9
172 Isaiah 41:10

We don't lose anything by running to God, seeking his help, and depending on his strengths. We gain peace, confidence, and rewards for trusting him and letting him be in charge. Life on Earth is a journey full of tests and challenges. Sometimes God puts people in tough situations where they can't do anything without his help. But God also prepares people to walk through tough times. When people are not prepared, they respond with worries and anxiety. Knowing that we do not belong to this world, we can understand why this world hates us and is full of ugly things, and it will always reject those who try to live differently by obeying God.

Anxieties and worries mess with people's belief systems and are the Devil's way of pushing people far from God. God did not give us the spirit of fear or worry. Jesus said, "That is why I tell you not to worry about everyday life."[173] We have to trust God for our everyday life. Fear blinds people's minds, and without a clear vision, they are lost, confused, and incapable of discerning right from wrong. People lose concentration in prayer or meditation. It's important to identify the signs of worry, anxiety, and loneliness and fight them with faith and God's help before it is too late.

The Devil is driving people crazy. He is using more conflicts and confusion, pushing people to do more evil and run far from God's presence. We have to wake up and fight back. It is written, "Humble yourselves before God. Resist the Devil and he will flee from you. Come close to God, and God will come close to you."[174] In Jesus, people have strength to identify the Devil's poisoning arrow, to resist him and to win. Life is a process full of good and tough times. But in bad times, we don't have to allow fear to dominate our mind and spirit. We don't have to be afraid but just call upon the name of the Lord; he will give us the strength, faith, and courage to overcome it. Tough times don't last; they always pass.

The apostle James wrote, "When trouble comes your way, consider it an opportunity for great joy. For you know that when your faith is tested, your endurance has a chance to grow. So let it grow, for when your endurance is fully developed, you will be perfect and complete, needing nothing."[175] In times of trouble, God is by our side to help and fight for us. He will never

---

173 Luke 12:22
174 James 4:7–8
175 James 1:2–4

let down those who put their trust in him. The psalmist said, "But even the best years are filled with pain and trouble; soon they disappear, and we fly away."[176]Turn to God when you feel helpless and he will fill you with his love and peace. Focus on God's promises even when you don't feel like it, and he will fill you with hope and give you the strength and passion to start all over again. The time and years of blessing are to come. God said, "But forget all that, it is nothing compared to what I am going to do; for I am about to do something new. See, I have already begun! Do you not see it?"[177] Forget the trouble and pain of the past; the years to come are rich in blessing and joy. Let yourself trust God's words.

When people mess up and feel lost and alone, those near to them, with love and compassion, have to encourage them and help them build their faith up and remind them they are not alone and that God still loves them. If together we pray and believe that God is able to do anything, healing and restoration will come upon those who need it. Jesus said, "Keep asking and it will be given to you. Keep searching, and you will find. Keep knocking, and the door will be opened to you. For everyone who asks receives, and the one who searches finds and to the one who knocks, the door will be opened."[178]It's never too late to come close to God, and it's not bad to insist on and be determined to reach God's blessing. In the gospel of Luke, Jesus asks, "Will not God grant justice to His elect who cry out to Him day and night? Will He delay to help them? I tell you that He will swiftly grant them justice."[179] God is good and just; he will always give comfort to his people. Jesus told people to be persistent and continuously search for God. He said, "But I tell you this, though He won't do it for friendship's sake, if you keep knocking long enough, He will get up and give you whatever you need because of your shameless persistence."[180] It is easy to quit and to give up when times are hard, but those who persevere and persist will be granted whatever they look and ask for.

Jesus is the reason people have to avoid fear and worry. He said, "I am leaving you with a gift, peace of mind and heart. And the peace I give is

---

176 Psalm 90:10b
177 Isaiah 43:18–19
178 Matthew 7:7–8
179 Luke 18:7
180 Luke 11:8

a gift the world cannot give. So don't be troubled or afraid."[181] In him we trust and have confidence that we will win any challenge because it is not by our strength but by his strength. With his name and power everything will be fine. The apostle Paul wrote, "Love never gives up, never loses faith, is always hopeful, and endures through every circumstance."[182]With love, faith, patience, courage, and perseverance we will win life's battles. God will never leave or forsake us. The righteous shall pass by tribulation, but in the name of Jesus, they will overcome it all. The prophet Jeremiah said, "But blessed are those who trust in the Lord and have made the Lord their hope and confidence."[183] Those who put their hope and confidence in the Lord shall find rest and peace. It is written, "If you make the Lord your refuge, if you make the Most High your shelter, no evil will conquer you; no plague will come near your home; for he will order his angels to protect you wherever you go."[184]We have learned in this second part that

- Jesus is the only way, the only truth, and the resurrection of life. He is the strength that people need to overcome evil. Without Jesus there is not salvation. Only Jesus's blood has the power to redeem people and allow them to approach the holy throne of God Almighty.

- The Holy Spirit is our partner and the power of God inside us. It guides and brings light and confidence within us. It empowered people to win the flesh and the world. With it we know where we came from, where we are, and where we are going.

- We learned five basic requirements that will help people build a solid and successful relationship of love and faith with God.

---

181 John 14:27
182 1 Corinthians 13:7
183 Jeremiah 17:7
184 Psalm 91:9–11

PART THREE:

GET READY FOR THE SECOND COMING

Chapter 9:

The Revelation of the Vision

"I would not have told the people of Israel to seek me if I could not be found. I, the Lord, speak only what is true and declare only what is right," said the Lord.

——Isaiah 45:19b—c

The Spirit of the Lord showed me a vision, but I didn't understand it in the beginning, and when God asked me to write this book, I didn't know how and where to start. I am not a pastor and have never gone to any Bible college. But by faith I obeyed and sat before my computer and asked the Holy Spirit to tell me what I should write. Obeying and humbling ourselves to God's will are the keys to seeing God's Spirit in action. From that point, the Spirit of the Lord was faithful. He guided me and the inspiration came upon me, and I wrote everything I heard from him. In the process of learning, writing, and meditating on the word of God, I began to understand and receive God's revelations about this vision.

The first part of this book helps us understand God's plan for his people. As I write, I understand that without people knowing their roots of suffering, weakness, and failures and without being conscious of their blindness, they will not understand or take seriously the second part of the book, which is about salvation and God's divine intervention of love to give them freedom, strength, and the weapons they need to win any battle in this world. This last part reveals the meaning of the vision and reminds people that God is still in charge and has the power to protect those who trust him and stay in his will even in times of trouble such as this. The message of the book has a purpose of preparing God's children for what is to come and to call them to be on the alert and ready for the coming of our Lord and Savior Jesus Christ.

The People in the Sky

Who are those people I saw in the vision, living in the sky and clothed in write? Those people are not angels or divine creatures. They are people like us, of different colors and from different nations and living on Earth, but cleansed and covered by Jesus's blood and protected by God's army of angels. Those people live an extraordinary spiritual life. They have received Jesus as their Lord and Savior, and he cleanses their sins and gives them his peace. They accept it and trust and obey him. The Holy Spirit lives within them and has become their partner and best friend, making them strong, powerful, and happy people. It is written, "For you were slaughtered, and your blood has ransomed people for God from every tribe and language and people for God and nation."[185] In the vision they were wearing white clothes and their faces were brilliant. The color white symbolizes God's holiness. The blood of the Lamb makes them holy, pure, brilliant, and special. Their faces were radiant because of the presence of God among them. In the book of Revelation it is written, "They have washed their robes in the blood of the Lamb and made them white. That is why they stand in front of God's throne and serve him day and night in his temple. And he who sits on the throne will give them shelter."[186] Those people are called to become priests and ministers of God, and they reign on the Earth.

Those people were sinners, liars, criminals, prostitutes, and thieves; they were sick, poor, and rejected and ignored by this world. Their minds were corrupted, their hearts were full of evil desires, and they were all driven to death. But one day, Jesus reached them, showed them love, opened their eyes with truth, changed their course, and gave them hope, forgiveness, and new hearts. Then they decided to follow God's rules and believe in Jesus. They gave their lives as sacrifice and as an act of thanksgiving for God's glory. They passed by tribulation, distress, persecution, and suffering, but

---

185 Revelation 5:9b
186 Revelation 7:14c–15

they remained faithful, obedient, and determined to honor God's word. Yes, those people will reign forever with Jesus.

Jesus said, "For from within, out of people's hearts, come evil thoughts, sexual immoralities, thefts, murders, adulteries, greed, evil actions, deceits, lewdness, stinginess, blasphemy, pride, and foolishness. All these evil things come from within and defile a person."[187] Jesus came to rescue man's evil heart by giving him a new one. With compassion and love, Jesus ransomed people for God. He made a new race of people empowered by the authority of his name to serve in the kingdom of God.

The apostle Paul was Saul the killer who did not search to know Jesus or to serve him, but one day Jesus reached him by his grace and changed the course of his life. Jesus changed his name and his heart, and Saul became Paul, the powerful man of God. In the book of Acts it is written, "God gave Paul the power to perform unusual miracles. When handkerchiefs or aprons that had merely touched his skin were placed on sick people, they were healed of their diseases, and evil spirits were expelled."[188] The apostle Paul was a powerful instrument in God's hands.

There is another man in the Bible who was ignored and rejected by his community. His family couldn't do anything to help him because he was possessed by demons and tormented by the spirit of darkness. Apostle Mark wrote about him and said, "Day and night he wandered among the burial caves and in the hills, howling and cutting himself with sharp stones."[189] But one day Jesus remembered him and traveled from the other side of the lake to where the possessed man was, just to deliver him and set him free from those evil spirits.

That man was amazed to see what Jesus did for him and begged Jesus to let him go with him, but Jesus said, "No, go home to your family, and tell them everything the Lord has done for you and how merciful he has been."[190] Jesus sent him to testify how he was forgotten by men but remembered by the Lord. Many people have testimonies of what Jesus has done for them. Some people have died and been brought back to life by God with messages and testimonies from God to people on Earth. Those

---

187 Mark 7:21
188 Acts 19:11–12
189 Mark 5:5
190 Mark 5:19

people are among us and have been set apart to testify to the world about the wonderful miracles Jesus has performed for them. They have a mission to bring sinners and nations back to the light of God. God doesn't want anyone to perish but to have eternal life.

Jesus said, "Look, I have given you authority over the power of the enemy, and you can walk among snakes and scorpions and crush them. Nothing will injure you."[191] Those people in the sky are merely humans like us. God has given them a second chance, and they didn't take it for granted. They repented from their sins and have the grace to be chosen by God to serve him. God made them able to preach and perform miracles and signs for his glory. They use God's Spirit to serve and to show God's love and power. No weapon forged against them can prosper. The invisible hand of God keeps them safe and protected on the Earth.

The apostle Paul said, "So we don't look at the trouble we can see now, rather, we fix our gaze on things that we cannot see. For things we see now will soon be gone, but the things we cannot see will last forever."[192] Those people in the sky are messengers from God. They live for God and don't look at the present trouble; they focus on their future in Jesus with great joy. They wait patiently and have confidence in God's promises and are prepared for the coming of their Lord and Savior, who will bring them to the wonderful land and reward them for doing a faithful job. Things we see will be gone sooner or later, but God and his words will last forever.

The Meaning of the Jump Rope

In the vision, I saw each one of those people in the sky throwing a jump rope down to the Earth. I asked myself what the jump rope represented and why it wasn't burned by the fire. The jump ropes represent the covenant of protection between God and people, and between people and people. The jump rope brings people to a high level with God and each jump rope represents Jesus Christ. People hold the jump ropes for protection and no one attach on that jump rope can perish. The people in the sky were sharing Jesus with others and calling people to light and life. They were extending their hands to people on Earth and sharing the good news of hope in Jesus. The people in the sky had the jump ropes attached to their

191 Luke 10:19
192 2 Corinthians 4:18

hands, but the people on Earth had to grab it and wait to be pulled up by them to the sky.

People need Jesus and need others to learn, to grow, and to succeed. Nobody can do anything on his or her own in this life without someone else's help. Those on high have to push up those who are down. The jump ropes are the connection and the power that both people in the sky and on Earth needed to accomplish their mission and goal. Their unity comes from the jump ropes. Jesus said, "I am in them and you are in me. May they experience such perfect unity that the world will know that you sent me and that you love them as much as you love me."[193] In the kingdom of Jesus, the strongest are those who practice the word of God and learn to use God's power for good purpose. The weakest are those who don't believe and are still under the power of the enemy. So the strongest have to extend their hands to the weakest and encourage them to trust God and win the challenge of this life and reach their highest potential. Those who are strong have the obligation to drive the blind and the lost to life and together in unity glorify God.

Jesus's work is a missionary service, and every believer is an ambassador of Christ, wherever he or she lives. Jesus's true follower has to preach by example, practicing and proving to the world that Jesus is what he said he is and the word of God is truth; that is how unbelievers around the world will come to the light. The good news has to be preached; sinners have to know that they are forgiven, there is not condemnation for those who come to Christ, and the gate of the kingdom of light still opens to anyone who freely comes to Jesus. He is the only way to eternal life.

To grab that jump rope, the people on the Earth have to look up, so they can be helped. Many people are not looking up for help. There are many men and women of God among us throwing their jump ropes every day to help people receive Jesus as Lord and Savior. It is written, "You should know that whoever brings back a sinner from wandering will save the sinner's soul from death and will cover a multitude of sins."[194] The word of God is available to anyone who wants to know Jesus. Spend your energy and time seeking the kingdom of God and eternal life will be given to you. Here on Earth we have received salvation and are waiting for God

193 John 17:23
194 James 5:20

to deliver us forever from the darkness and to bring us to the new land of peace and happiness.

We have to help others open their spiritual eyes, renounce their evil ways, and repent and choose the eternal life given by Jesus. Our mission begins with families, close friends, neighbors, and everywhere. This vision reminds us that we have to evangelize more and persist in telling the truth until the Lord returns. In his letter to Timothy, the apostle Paul said, "Proclaim the message, persist in it whether convenient or not; rebuke, correct, and encourage with great patience and teaching.[195]" Every Christian has to throw his jump rope, lead by example, and make the word of God practicable and real. The people in the sky were also sharing their testimonies and teaching others how to get up there with them. Today if you read this book, listen, obey, and take my jump rope that I offer you in this book. Grab it and give Jesus a chance to save your life.

Whoever is touched by the Spirit of God is inspired to spread the good news of salvation all over the world and to glorify God for his goodness. It is time to take God's warning seriously. There is a room for everybody in God's house. Let the Spirit of God guide your heart to a safe place. Jesus said in the gospel of Matthew, "Go, therefore, and make disciples of all nations, baptizing them in the name of Father and the Son and of the Holy Spirit, teaching them to observe everything I have commanded you."[196] God's will is for everyone to enter his kingdom. People of every nation and tongue are welcome in Jesus's name.

In the parable of the rich man and Lazarus, the rich man after his death found himself in the place of torment. He begged Abraham, "Please, Father Abraham, at least send Lazarus to my father's home. For I have five brothers and I want him to warn them so they don't end up in this place of torment."[197] And Abraham responded, "Moses and the prophets have warned them. Your brother can read what they wrote."[198] Some of our loved ones who have passed away are looking down and would like to send to their brothers, sisters, and kids this message: "Please take the

---

195 2 Timothy 4:2
196 Matthew 28:19
197 Luke 16:27–28
198 Luke 16:29

jump ropes. Change and turn away from evil minds, and don't end in the place of torment."

For those who are still alive, there is still hope, and it is never too late for change. This is the time to make the right decision and give Jesus a chance to change your circumstances and your life. He will never deceive you. Jesus said, "Those who have done good will rise to experience eternal life, and those who have continued in evil will rise to experience judgment."[199] One day God will separate good people from this world and every evil thing will be destroyed and every good thing will be taken with God. What side will you be on? It is time to know for sure that Jesus knows you and whether your name is written in the book of the Lamb of God.

People who served good and loved God will live through eternity with God. Those who have served evil will live through eternity in the lake of fire with the Devil. Noah and Lot prepared and advised people about the destruction, but the people didn't believe them and were destroyed. I have delivered this message to advise people that God doesn't want them to perish; he wants them to be awake and to accept the jump rope (Jesus) and turn away from the evil side.

The end and the destruction of evil is about to happen. Only those who are under Jesus's protection will be safe and taken with him into his kingdom. Make the right decision now of putting God first, and wait patiently and with great joy the spectacular return of the Lord Jesus.

Ugly Faces

In the vision I saw ugly faces with mouths of fire. They were between the Earth and the sky. They always appeared when someone took the jump rope and began to go up. Those ugly faces represent the Devil and the ugliness of the spirit of darkness. There is a war going on between light and darkness. Every time someone decides to reject the work of darkness and join the light of God, he will be intimidated and attacked by the force of darkness. Those ugly faces were there to intimidate, to mess with people's minds, and to try to block their passage to the sky. They were only attacked those who touched the jump ropes and tried to go up. People

---

199 John 6:29

who give their life to Jesus and want to grow spiritually will face those ugly creatures always.

Every time believers want to please God and do the right thing, the Devil will show his true ugly side to scare and discourage them. He always puts up obstacles and intimidations to create doubt and to mess with their belief systems. People have to know that the Devil is attacking them, not because of where they have been or where they are but for where they are going. So be smart: do not let the Devil stop you from becoming who God predestined you to become. Pursue the course and reach your final destination.

Today people give permission for fear, discouragement, and worry to enter their hearts and make them easily quit on God. That is because of lack of knowledge, trust, and confidence in God's words. God never denied the presence of the Devil or said people would not be tempted by or attacked by the Devil. But he assures people that he will be there to protect them and show his power and make everything possible for those who trust him and stay in his will.

People's power or weakness comes from their belief systems. Those people who believe in the high power of God have the ability to conquer anything and succeed in everything they do. But those who don't believe in God's power are weak, defeated, and easily manipulated by the Devil. Worry and fear come from the Devil's blindness. The manifestation of worries and fear in people means they don't trust God with their life and that they believe the Devil has the power to do what he wants to them. Without hope, those kinds of people are miserable.

Those who believe in Jesus have to have confidence in his love and power to save them. They are not powerless and are not alone. Their hope is in Jesus, their Savior and Lord. Even when the Devil tries to show up in their ways, they will not be afraid and will trust God to deliver them. It is written, "Do not be afraid for I have ransomed you. I have called you by name; you are mine. When you go through deep water, I will be with you. When you go through rivers of difficulty, you will not drown. When you walk through the fire of oppression, you will not be burned up; for I am the Lord your God, the Holy One of Israel, your Savior."[200]The Devil doesn't have the power to undo what God has done. We can't lose faith and must

---

200 Isaiah 43:1–3

put effort, trust, and discipline into our walk with God. Those who resist the Devil will get to the secret place and enjoy life. In the vision, the fire from the ugly creatures did not have the power to burn the jump ropes or the people holding on to them. Those ugly creatures were screaming aloud. They were furious and sent more fire from their mouths, but nothing happened to those who remained holding on to the jump ropes. The Devil and his demons didn't have the power to touch those attached to Jesus and covered by his holy blood.

I saw courageous people closing their eyes, ignoring the ugly faces with their fire and screams, determined to get to the sky. They knew that they were being attacked for going to that beautiful place, and they were determined to get there with the help of those who were pulling them up. They held on to the jump rope no matter what they saw and faced in the way. In their minds, they decided to die rather than give up on hope. The apostle Paul said, "We think you ought to know, dear brothers and sisters, about the trouble we went through in the province of Asia. We were crushed and overwhelmed beyond our ability to endure, and we thought we would never live through it. In fact, we expected to die. But as a result, we stopped relying on ourselves and learned to rely only on God, who raises the dead. And he did rescue us from mortal danger, and he will rescue us again. We have placed our confidence in him, and he will continue to rescue us."[201] The secret of passing through those ugly faces is found in Paul's testimony. He and other disciples faced dangers and death, but they stopped relying on their own understanding, embraced their faith in God's words, and relied only on God's strength. They remained confident in God's promises. Jesus said, "So you cannot become my disciple without giving up everything you own."[202] People who choose God's side have to surrender everything they own to him and put God in first place. Nothing can separate God from those who remain faithful to him.

It is written, "And I am convinced that nothing can ever separate us from God's love. Neither death nor life, neither angels nor demons, neither our fears for today nor our worries about tomorrow; not even the powers of hell can separate us from God's love."[203] Nothing that the Devil uses

---

201 2 Corinthians 1:8–10
202 Luke 14:33
203 Romans 8:38

has the power to separate God from his people. In Jesus, people are holy and have the power to win in any circumstances. Even when the passage to reach the blessing is full of trials and pains, we have to remain strong, relying on God's words and focusing more on where God is bringing us. We have to trust God and place our confidence in his promises. In his letter to the Hebrews, Apostle Paul gives us this valuable lesson: "Since Jesus has gone through suffering and testing, he is able to help us when we are being tested."[204]No matter how bad the situation may look, we have to stay faithful and attached to Jesus. In this vision, people passed through hard times, but those who didn't give up reached the sky. Their example of faith and courage has to give us hope and strength to continue our course to heaven. If they complete their course and win, we can, too. We should imitate their faith in Jesus.

I was praying and cheering in my heart for those who resisted and didn't give up and reached the sky. But in the vision, only a few people reached the sky. When they reached there, a loud shout of victory came from my mouth, and I saw those people in the sky rejoicing, too, with songs and praise. It is a blessing to rejoice in spirit with victorious people. People have to realize that they have been blinded, manipulated, and used as instruments by the Devil for a long time. It is time to be awake, to return in the right direction, and to put our hope and trust in God, who has the power to save and deliver.

This is the time to stand together and learn how to love, to forgive, to care, and to protect the human race. God did not create people to hurt other people but to love and care. If all the people of the world made peace with God and with themselves and joined in their efforts to fight the Devil and wisely denied him access to their hearts, becoming doorkeeper and protector for each other, life on Earth could be better, like in heaven.

Scared People

I saw people who were going up, panicked as they saw the scary and ugly faces. Some let go of the jump rope and were killed by the ugly faces. It was sad. They were going in the right direction, but they died because they detached themselves from the jump rope, which was their power and

---

204 Hebrew 2:18

protection. Other people held on to the jump ropes, but because of fear, they decided to return quickly to Earth. Once on Earth they let go of the jump ropes and became confused and powerless.

Then I remember that Jesus said, "Work hard to enter the narrow door to God's kingdom, for many will try to enter but will fail."[205] The scared people tried but failed. Others were killed because they didn't have enough faith and focused more on the attackers; giving those ugly faces power and letting them destroy their life. The ugly creatures killed them without pity. What a sad ending. It is written in Psalm, "I shall not die, but I shall live, and recount the deeds of the Lord."[206]When people focus more on trouble and circumstances than on hearing God, they don't realize that they are giving permission to the Devil to hurt and kill them. The Devil can't do anything if we don't give him access, and when he enters without compassion or mercy, he destroys and kills. He is a rebel and a terrorist. He will use every opportunity that he has to bring confusion, doubt, and anxiety to people's lives. The Devil makes people weak, vulnerable, and sick. He steals peace, hope, and God's words in people's minds, making their lives miserable. The apostle Paul said in the letter to Timothy, "For God has not given us a spirit of fear and timidity, but of power, love, and self-discipline."[207] Fear doesn't come from God but from the Devil. God gives us power and the strength to overcome fear and resist the Devil.

People have to know that Jesus fought the Devil and won. The Devil has been judged and the time will come when he will be thrown into the lake of fire. People have to be prepared and take all the weapons of God and refuse to follow the Devil. Many people wonder why life is so difficult and challenging on Earth. It is because of the dark force of the Devil, which has a mission to blind, confuse, distract, and make it difficult for people to find true happiness and peace of mind. It takes faith, love, discipline, passion, and real dedication to stay connected to God's promises and to get out from under the Devil's control.

In the vision the people who returned to Earth were miserable, divided between good and evil. They were unstable and undecided. They wanted what God had to offer but didn't want to make sacrifices and trust God

---

205 Luke 13:24
206 Psalm 118:19
207 2 Timothy 1:7

with their lives and surrender everything to him. They didn't have the courage to face obstacles and pain and to believe that God was able to deliver them from any trouble. Those scared people always have excuses to not progress. They always complain and murmur and blame God for their failures. Their minds are blind, and they live under the Devil's fear.

The apostle Paul said, "Satan, who is the god of this world, has blinded the minds of those who don't believe."[208] The influence of the Devil pushes those people to do more evil, and in their despair, they create false religions. The prophet Jeremiah wrote this: "O Lord, the hope of Israel. All who turn away from you will be disgraced. They will be buried in the dust of the Earth, for they have abandoned the Lord, the fountain of living water."[209] Man's religion is limited and deceives people. It gives short relief and teaches false ideologies. Their gods are false and can't give them eternal life.

Other kinds of people are rebels and proud. They don't want God to tell them what to do. They don't understand that if God doesn't, the Devil will. What God says saves people, and what the Devil says destroys and kills. God is life and the Devil is death. Life is a battle between good and evil. The goodness of God drives good people to happiness and to light, and the evil side drives evil people to sadness and darkness. If people listen to God, they will survive, but if they listen to the Devil, they will collapse and die. The door of heaven is still open to anyone who wants to repent and come back to God. God is merciful and faithful to those who humble themselves and need his help. Those who decide to come back to God will be welcomed and rescued.

Other kinds of people focus more on the outside appearance of thing or people and judge others by the color of their skin. God is invisible. It is difficult for these kinds of people to believe or trust him because they don't know how he looks. These people spend time and energy working on their looks and their appearances but neglect their spirits. They want to give people a false image of what they are not, making people believe that they are happy, but when nobody is around; they feel lonely, empty, and miserable. They can't sleep and don't have peace of mind.

---

208 1 Corinthians 4:4
209 Jeremiah 17:13

When people understand that God is Spirit and that only his Spirit can give people power and strength to overcome anything, they will focus and take care of their spirits first. The inner person has the power to take care of or destroy the body. If it is happy and prosperous, the body will follow it, but if it is frustrated, poor, and unhappy, the body will follow that, too. We have to spend more time and effort on our inner person and educate our spirit to obey and follow God's guidance. Those who surrender their life to God and believe that his Spirit resides inside them will honor him and be protected wherever they go, and they will prosper in every aspect of their life. They will have peace and will rest in the shadow of the mighty God. Every day, he will nourish their spirit and fill them with joy and strength.

This is the time of decision. Choose life and accept God's love, grace, mercy, help, power, and salvation. His house is huge and big enough to contain every nation. There is a place for everyone. Dear brothers and sisters open your hearts and receive God's gifts of life. The psalmist wrote, "This is the gate of the Lord. The righteous shall enter through it."[210] So I invite everybody to reconcile with God through Jesus and give him a chance to change our past behavior and give us new hearts and good spirits. This is what God said: "As surely as I live, says the Sovereign Lord, I take no pleasure in the death of wicked people. I only want them to turn from their wicked ways so they can live. Turn! Turn from your wickedness, O people of Israel! Why should you die?"[211] No one has to be left behind.

This is not the time for distractions but time to take God's word seriously. Let's let Jesus clean our hearts and help us turn away from wicked ways. We have to search for God's wisdom and have a sincere relationship of trust with him. God has given everyone the opportunity to receive eternal life in Jesus Christ and live. Let's focus on where God is taking us and wait with joy for our rewards. The apostle Paul wrote, "Therefore we do not give up; even though our outer person is being destroyed, our inner person is being renewed day by day. For our momentary light affliction is producing for us an absolutely incomparable eternal weight of glory."[212] The

---

210 Psalm 118:20
211 Ezekiel 33:11
212 2 Corinthians 4:16–17

afflictions on Earth are momentary. But if we don't take this opportunity to run to God, we will be thrown out into the eternal affliction of hell.

A long time ago Moses said to God's people, "This command I am giving you today is not too difficult for you to understand, and it is not beyond your reach. It is not kept in heaven, so distant that you must ask: who will go up to heaven and bring it down so we can hear it and obey? It is not kept beyond the sea, so far away that you must ask: who will cross the sea to bring it to us so we can hear it and obey? No, the message is very close at hand; it is on your lips and in your heart so that you can obey it."[213]God's word is our treasure; it is available and accessible to everyone. His Spirit is within us to help and empower us. Moses is telling us today to choose life by obeying and trusting God's instructions. No more excuses. God has already provided everything for us to succeed and the Holy Spirit is our wonderful partner; he will guide people to the gate of heaven.

---

213 Deuteronomy 30:11–14

Chapter 10:

The Safety Zone of Protection

I will make a covenant of peace with my people and drive
away the dangerous animals from the land. Then they will
be able to camp safety in the wildest places and sleep in the
woods without fear.

——Ezekiel 34:25

In the vision I saw people in the sky. What is the spiritual meaning of the sky? The sky is a secret place where God guards and protects the true worshippers, those who worship him in truth and in spirit. God made a covenant with them that if they search for him, he will help them reach that place where they will no longer suffer fear or disappointments. He will give them peace, prosperity, security, and rest. It's a place where God drives away the Devil and his demons, and where people don't worry any more about anything because God provides everything for them.

A long time ago, before Jesus, God's people were worshipping him in places such as a mountain or in a special city such as Jerusalem. Jesus said to a woman, "Woman, believe me, the hour is coming when you will worship the Father neither on this mountain nor in Jerusalem,"[214] and he said, "But the hour is coming, and is now here, when the true worshipers will worship the Father in spirit and truth, for the Father seeks such as these to worship Him. God is Spirit, and those who worship Him must worship in spirit and truth."[215]The sky is a spiritual state of worship. It is a

---

214 John 4:21
215 John 4:23–24

spiritual place where people worship God in truth and spirit. People don't need mountains or special cities to worship God anymore. Everywhere or anywhere, people can worship God because God is Spirit and can be found everywhere. God is omnipotent and omnipresent. Those who adore and love with all their hearts must worship him in spirit and truth. God wants to be in touch with people, and the only way to connect with him is by faith in spirit and truth.

Jesus came to save spirits and souls. He was concerned more about the inner person and their eternal rest, where they will live forever. He wants to give the inner person power and authority over the outside world. To understand Jesus, people have to open their minds and prepare themselves to receive spiritual truth and not a human point of view. Jesus said to his disciples, "To you it has been given to know the secret of the Kingdom; but to others I speak in parables, so that the looking but not perceiving and listening but not understanding."[216] The true worshippers nourish their spirits with God's word every day. The more they learn, the more they grow and the more power they have. With God's strength and power they crucify their flesh and desires and live a holy life. It is written, "Live by the Spirit, I say, and do not gratify the desires of the flesh."[217] The flesh pushes people to do what they want, but the Spirit pushes people to do what God wants. The flesh and its desires drive people to death, but the Spirit drives people to eternal life. God's word gives people understanding and wisdom to live a quiet, peaceful life. True prosperity comes from the inside out. That means from our inner person (our spirit), to our flesh (our thinking), to our body (our exterior appearance). The apostle John wrote, "Dear friends, I hope all is well with you and that you are as healthy in body as you are strong in spirit."[218] When people live by spirit, they produce spiritual fruits, which are love, joy, peace, patience, kindness, generosity, faithfulness, gentleness, and self-control. Every fruit of Spirit that people bear is like a step higher toward the safe place. Every fruit earned is a key that opens a security gate that brings people to heaven. The more fruits earned, the more keys received and the closer people are to reaching the place of safety. People have to bear all those spiritual fruits and continuously

---

216 Luke 8:10
217 Galatians 5:16
218 3 John 2

progress toward the perfection of God. The spiritual life is a journey full of good and bad experiences that make people learn and grow. It is a process and a wonderful journey, because with every step, God's people discover more about God and receive more blessing.

Every child of God has to pursue the perfection of God to gain true prosperity and spiritual strength. People are not perfect, but God is, and in Jesus, people are made perfect. We don't have perfection because we don't ask for it or believe it is possible. God gives to those who ask. King Solomon asked for wisdom, and God gave him more than wisdom. It is written, "So God replied, because you have asked for wisdom in governing my people with justice and have not asked for a long life or wealth or the death of your enemies, I will give you a wise and understanding heart such as no one else has had or ever will have."[219] King Solomon had what he asked for and more, because he humbled himself before God and recognized that without God's help he couldn't govern a nation.

God wants people to acknowledge his love, his richness, and his kindness, and come to him for help. God never hides his face and his presence from those who search for him and trust him. God is using wonderful people today to help and encourage others based on their own experience. All God's people have experienced his powerful hand in their lives and are more than happy to share it with others. There have always been ups and downs in their lives, but they never stopped trusting and holding Jesus in their hearts. In the vision I saw them in the sky helping, encouraging, and teaching others to walk in faith and to trust God to reach the safety zone where every child of God has to be.

Accepting Jesus is the most important step and the foundation upon which people will build their faith and success in their spiritual journey. If that foundation is solid, it will stand whenever winds come, and not fall. But if it is not solid, at the first challenge, it will fall and be destroyed. We have to understand from the beginning of our relationship with Christ why we commit and make a covenant with God through Jesus. That will help people stay confident and pursue their course to victory. Everybody needs God and has to search for his help to win any challenge. God doesn't need anything from people, He alone is God. All he wants is to see people happy and thankful for what he does and will do for them. He is offering

---

219 1 Kings 3:11–12

happiness, peace, and life for free, but there is an enemy whose job is to steal those gifts from God and kill people.

If people are not prepared and don't have a good understanding of how things work in the spiritual world, they will collapse and quit at the first challenge. The Devil always tries to steal the seed of God in people's spirit and presents them with perishable and false happiness. For those who are strong, the Devil brings difficulties and challenges to see if they will resist and will still love and commit to God. But through those trials and troubles, faith is being tested and slowly people are earning spiritual maturity and moving forward to the safety zone of God. Testing develops spiritual character and confidence in God's promises. All great men and women of God pass through times of testing and difficulties, but they hold on to God's promises. They wait patiently for God's answers, endure with faith their testing, reach their blessing, and become prosperous.

Trials and suffering can't stop people from having hope in God's promises. Nothing has the power to make God's people quit or give up on him. People who reached the sky have grown through endurance. They passed by the ugly creatures, they endured their testing, and with Jesus on their side, they completed their course with victory. Testing qualified them for the high spiritual level. God blesses those who patiently endure testing and temptation. He surrounds them with his arms of love and fights for them day and night.

The psalmist said, "There are glad songs of victory in the tents of the righteous: the right hand of the Lord does valiantly."[220] Worship and praise are always in the mouths of the redeemers because God changes their course to death, becoming their source, and brings them to a life of happiness and peace. He gives them his Spirit and makes them righteous. When people look back and see how God delivered them and fought for them, songs of praise and victory come out of their mouths to thank God for everything. In the spiritual stage of praising, people don't worry any more about trials and difficulties; they pray and praise God for good or for bad. The presence of God is everything they need all the time. The peace of God in their heart makes them able to listen without doubting to the voice of God and receive his revelations.

---

220 Psalm 118:15

This is an illustration of how to get to that place of safety called sky. It is like traveling in an airplane. Many people when traveling by airplane have to decide to trust the pilot and believe that they will get to their destination. When people take their seats inside the airplane, the doors are closed and no one can get out anymore. People put their safety belts on before the airplane takes off and when it is landing. As the airplane begins to take off, everything seen through the airplane window becomes smaller, and as the airplane gets more altitude, everything disappears.

But when the airplane reaches cruising speed, people don't need their safety belts anymore. They are free to move, eat, and rest. The cruising altitude is the altitude at which the pilot, the crew, and the passengers can enjoy the trip and relax because it is the safety zone. Any pilot or airplane specialist will tell you that the possibility of an airplane crashing is higher when it is taking off or landing. To avoid accidents, the pilot has to use maximum power and use more precautions to make the airplane take off or land. But when the airplane reaches cruising altitude, the pilot relaxes and uses fewer controls with less effort.

This illustration is an example of what happens in the spiritual life with Jesus. When people take a first step into Christian life, trials and difficulties seem like they will never end, but they have to persist and put on their safety belt, which is their faith in God's word, and continue to go higher and higher to reach that place where trials and difficulties seem small and without power over their spiritual life. When we know God better, we trust him more and feel the desire to honor and serve him with all our heart forever.

The word of God is the safety belt that we need to remain focused on and attached to in time of trouble. People need more strength and faith in their period of testing. They have to spend more time with God in prayer. They have to trust their pilot, the Holy Spirit of God. He will help them have security and confidence, and continue their course. It is written, "Those who listen to instruction will prosper; those who trust the Lord will be joyful."[221] Trust, commitment, time, effort, patience, and persistence are tools that people need to use to reach the safety zone of protection. In that place, the presence of God brings joy, peace, and strength to win the challenges of life, and nothing has power there to steal peace or joy

---

221 Proverbs 16:20

in the heart of God's people. The apostle Paul said, "We are pressed on every side by trouble, but we are not crushed. We are perplexed, but not driven to despair. We are hunted down, but never abandoned by God. We get knocked down, but we are not destroyed."[222] For people who reach the safety zone, tough times are less important; what matters for them is their commitment to serving God. Trials and sorrows will always exist on this journey, but as we grow in faith, they will become smaller and insignificant because our focus is on God's words and promises. Jesus said, "I have told you all this so that you may have peace in me. Here on the Earth you will have many trials and sorrows. But take heart, because I have overcome the world."[223] The safety zone is where we rest in peace with God's word and enjoy his blessing because Jesus has overcome the challenges of this world for us.

It is written in Psalm, "The Lord says: I will rescue those who love me. I will protect those who trust in my name. When they call on me, I will answer; I will be with them in trouble, I will rescue and honor them. I will reward them with a long life and give them my salvation."[224] The reward is for those who prosper in spirit and remain focused on the will of God for their life. People who are living according to the truth are prosperous. In Psalm it is written, "They are like trees planted along the riverbank, bearing fruit each season. Their leaves never wither, and they prosper in all they do."[225] Jesus is a riverbank where flows living water that makes those who are planted along him bear fruit each season. Wherever they do and touch it will prosper. It is written, "God keeps such people so busy enjoying life that they take no time to brood over the past."[226] We can start well with the Lord, but we have to stay good and end well. It is written, "Finishing is better than starting."[227] People have to stay in God's will forever. If they turn away, they will lose everything. It is written, "For again I say, when righteous people turn away from their righteous behavior and turn to evil, they will die. But if wicked people turn from their wickedness and do what

---

222 2 Corinthians 4:8–9
223 John 16:33
224 Psalm 91:14–16
225 Psalm 1:3
226 Ecclesiastes 6:20
227 Ecclesiastes 7:8

is just and right, they will live."[228] We have to make a daily decision of remaining righteous forever. Our focus has to be on the final destination, which is the coming of our Lord and Savior Jesus Christ.

Be prepared, taught time are to come. The Devil is furious and wants to bring many people with him to hell, where he is destined for eternal death. One day, the Devil complained to God about Job and said, "You have always put a wall of protection around him and his home and his property; you have made him prosper in everything he does. Look how rich he is."[229] Then the Devil asked permission from God to cross the wall of protection to test Job's faith. Today the Devil doesn't have access to that wall of protection because of the blood of the Lamb that covers and protects God's people.

These last days will be tough on the Earth, but those who are hidden by Jesus's blood in the safe place will survive the Devil's anger. In this vision, God is inviting all his people to follow the Holy Spirit's guidance and to run with urgency to that security zone. People have to invest their time and efforts in searching God's will for their lives and obeying God's instructions. Love and faith in God's words are powerful weapons against the Devil and have to be the center of focus and attention for God's people. It is written, "For we live by believing and not by seeing."[230] God's people have to feed their spirits with more spiritual foods and became spiritually healthy.

All children of God need to enjoy life and reach the secret place that God has prepared for them. It is a place of peace with God and others. Nothing matters more there than the presence of God. When we are in that secret place, God protects us and makes us prosper and grow rich. In the safety zone of protection our job is to praise, to thank, to share, and to worship the Lamb of God. In Jesus everything is good and perfect. Jesus said, "Now that you know these things, God will bless you for practicing them."[231] If you hear God's voice today, choose life with God; open your heart, focus on his words, trust him, and let the Holy Spirit of God, who is

---

228 Ezekiel 33:18–19
229 Job 1:10
230 2 Corinthians 5:7
231 John 13:17

the pilot, fly you to God's secret place and make you ready for the second coming of the Messiah.

Chapter 11:

The Second Coming of Jesus Christ

He who is the faithful witness to all these things says: Yes, I am coming soon.

——Revelation 22:20

We are living the last days before God concludes the last chapter of his salvation's plan. The rescue of the Israelites in Egypt foreshadowed Jesus's coming to set God's people free from this world's slavery. Jesus promised to bring the faithful people to the Promised Land. Prophecies are being fulfilled. We are witnessing everything that it is written about the last days. It's a time of precaution. We have to be awake, alert, and prepared. At any time, the Lord can return. Only those who are not distracted will be able to see him coming in his glory.

Today people are lost in their daily routines and forget that Jesus said, "Watch out! Don't let your hearts be dulled by carousing and drunkenness and by the worries of this life. Don't let that day catch you unaware."[232] People shall continuously watch out, be on guard, and pray until Jesus returns. We can't miss our final destination. Jesus said, "Keep alert at all times. And pray that you might be strong enough to escape these coming horrors and stand before the Son of Man."[233] The athlete always wins the prize after he finishes the marathon. The Devil is turning around, searching for scared people, those who are weak and not strong in faith to distract, to destroy, and to kill them.

---

232 Luke 21:34
233 Luke 21:36

This what the prophet Daniel saw in a vision of the scenes of the last days: "There will be a time of distress such as never has occurred since nations came into being until that time. But at that time all your people who are found written in the book will escape. Many of those who sleep in the dust of the Earth will awake, some to eternal life, and some to shame and eternal contempt. Those who are wise will shine like the bright expanse of the heavens, and those who lead many to righteousness, will shine like the stars forever and ever."[234] Are we among those who are wise and will shine like the bright expanse of heaven and stars forever? If we are not, this is the time to become wise before it too late. The last days will be tough, but God advises his people to not be afraid because his wings of protection will cover them. God said to the prophet Daniel, "Go on your way, Daniel, for the words are secret and sealed until the time of the end. Many will be purified, cleansed, and refined, but the wicked will act wickedly; none of the wicked will understand, but the wise will understand."[235] Only the wise will understand this message from God and will change their wicked ways and return to God's house.

This is the time to purify, clean, refine, and be wise. Everyone has to be sure they are cleaned and purified by the blood of Jesus. Only through Jesus will people escape the tribulation of the last days. Jesus advised his people and said, "And when you hear of wars and insurrections, don't panic. Yes, these things must take place, but the end won't follow immediately. Then nation will go to war against nation, and kingdom against kingdom. There will be great earthquakes, and there will be famines and plagues in many lands, and there will be terrifying things and great miraculous signs from heaven."[236] When these things happen, recognize that the kingdom of God is near. Yes, the kingdom of God is near and Jesus is coming back like he promised.

He said, "Heaven and Earth will disappear, but my words will never disappear."[237] But while waiting for his coming, we have to be aware and wary of false messiahs and messages from the Antichrist. In the gospel of Matthew, Jesus said, "False messiahs and false prophets will arise and

234 Daniel 12:1–3
235 Daniel 12:9–10
236 Luke 21:9–11
237 Luke 21:33

perform great signs and wonders to lead astray, if possible, even the elect …
They will tell you: he's in the inner rooms! Do not believe it."[238] Jesus
warned us about them because he knows how they can lead people in the
wrong direction. People must read the word of God and search God by
themselves and trust the Holy Spirit of God inside them to lead them in
the right direction.

In the letter to the Thessalonians it is written, "Do not stifle the Holy
Spirit. Do not scoff at prophecies, but test everything that is said. Hold on
to what is good. Stay away from every kind of evil."[239] We have to be on
guard and alert so we will not be deceived. Jesus said in the gospel of John,
"I assure you: Anyone who hears my word and believes Him who sent me
has eternal life and will not come under judgment but has passed from
death to life. I assure you: An hour is coming and is now here, when the
dead will hear the voice of the Son of God, and those who hear will live …
Those who have done good things, to resurrection of the life, but those
who have done wicked things, to the resurrection of judgment."[240] The
time of separation of righteousness and wicked is near. Jesus said, "That
is the way it will be at the end of the world. The angels will come and
separate the wicked people from the righteous, throwing the wicked into
the fiery furnace, where there will be weeping and gnashing of teeth."[241]
The righteous will rejoice and the wicked will cry forever. God will take
away his people and everything that belongs to him: love, grace, mercy,
joy, light, and life. God's things that were protecting the Earth will be gone
forever and the Earth will collapse.

In these last days we don't have to worry about things that this world
offers, but we have to watch over our souls and spirits. Jesus said again,
"That day will come on you unexpectedly like a trap. For it will come on
all who live on the face of the whole Earth. But be alert at all times, praying
that you may have strength to escape all these things that are going to take
place and to stand before the Son of Man."[242] Jesus is coming soon. He said,
"And then at last, the sign that the Son of Man is coming will appear in
the heavens, and there will be deep mourning among all the people of the

238 Matthew 24:24
239 1 Thessalonians 5:19–22
240 John 5:24–29
241 Matthew 13:49–50
242 Luke 21:34:36

Earth. And they will see the Son of Man coming on the cloud of heaven with power and great glory."[243] Every eye will see him coming from heaven with his army of angels in power and glory. Jesus will take away those who have been resisting the Devil to the end. They will inherit everything with him. He will live with them in the holy city, the New Jerusalem.

God has prepared a beautiful city for his people. It written in the book of the prophet Isaiah, "For I will create a new heaven and a new Earth; the past events will not be remembered or come to mind. Then be glad and rejoice forever in what I am creating; for I will create Jerusalem to be a joy, and its people to be a delight. I will rejoice in Jerusalem and be glad in my people. The sound of weeping and crying will no longer be heard in her."[244] The new city doesn't need the sun or the moon to shine on it, because God's glory illuminates it and its lamp is the Lamb. Night will no longer exist, and people will not need lamplight or sunlight, because the Lord God will give them light. And they will reign forever and ever.

It is written in Revelation, "Look! God's dwelling is with men, and He will live with them. They will be His people. And God Himself will be with them and be their God. He will wipe away every tear from their eyes. Death will exist no longer; grief, crying, and pain will exist no longer, because the previous things have passed away."[245] But those who have chosen evil and whose names are not in the book of life will be thrown into hell with the Devil. In the book of Revelation it is written, "And anyone not found written in the book of life was thrown into the lake of fire."[246] This lake of fire is the second eternal death. No one deserves to be thrown there.

Please, take this opportunity to make things right with Jesus. This world is passing away, along with everything. But those who remain faithful to God will live forever. It is written, "Rejoice always, pray without ceasing, and give thanks in all circumstances; for this is the will of God in Christ Jesus for you."[247] This is an alert and a reminder from God. Jesus is coming soon at an hour that nobody knows. Be ready to stand before God's throne of glory. I am like a watchwoman; I sound the alarm to

---

243 Matthew 24:30
244 Isaiah 65:17–19
245 Revelation 21:3–4
246 Revelation 20:15
247 I Thessalonians 5:16–18

warn people to get ready. If you ignore it, the responsibility is yours, but if you listen, you will be protected by the mighty hand of the Lord, who will save your life.

It is written, "And He said to me: It is done! I am the Alpha and the Omega, the Beginning and the End."[248] Yes, the beginning and the end are coming. Amen.

We have learned in this last part that

- The Devil and his dark forces blind people and try to push them down and far away from God. He is trying to stop God's people from reaching God's place of safety.
- There is a secret place to which the righteous people have to run to have security, strength, peace, happiness, and blessing.
- We must be awake, prepared, and ready. Rejoice! Jesus is coming back soon. Don't be afraid and don't be alarmed. The end of evil is about to arrive.

---

248 Revelation 21:6

Conclusion

This is a wonderful book inspired by the Holy Spirit of the Lord to push us to the highest dimensions of spiritual life. We have learned about God, how he works, and how he has planned to save us since the first time sin entered our hearts. We learned also about Jesus the Son of God, who is the divine gift from God to people. He comes to save humanity from eternal death.

In the vision the Holy Spirit revealed the secret of reaching the safe zone of God. Through this vision everyone can identify his or her own identity. Some are people in the sky, enjoying God's favor. Others are on their way to the sky fighting the ugly creatures. Some others are the scared people who return and are lost on the Earth. Many others never paid attention to the jump rope falling on their heads to save them. They never heard the good news or took seriously God's warning. No matter who we are and where we are, we have works to do and missions to accomplish.

The strongest have to pull up the weakest and together unite in Jesus; we will empty the evil side and fill the heavens. This book helps people understand that by uniting with God, we are one and stronger than ever. When people come together obeying and trusting God, they have power to overcome anything and live a supernatural life. First we have to forgive, to reconcile, and to honor Jesus's name and continue his commission of going and making entire nations the disciples of Christ.

Life on Earth can be as peaceful and wonderful as it is in heaven only if God's people reunite their efforts for the purpose of honoring God and changing this world. Only God can give us the strength to live peacefully in these last days and protect people against the Devil. In God's presence people will be free to praise and glorify his mighty name and thank him for his goodness and salvation. This book is a wakeup call from God to all his people to be prepared and ready for what is to come. People have to take seriously God's advice and respect God's servants among them.

The Holy Spirit used parables and illustrations in this book to make it easier for people to understand this message from God. We have to meditate on the word of God day and night and live the holy life as Christ did. Do not follow the advice of the wicked. Reach the lost and bring them to light. Serve the Lord with reverent fear and rejoice in his presence. Jesus is coming soon. This is the time to wash our dirty clothes and be ready to live with him for eternity. Jesus said, "Put your trust in the light while there is still time; then you will become children of the light."[249] Again this is the time to watch and be on the alert. Do not let any distractions make you miss the Second Coming of the Messiah. Once again, he is coming soon.

People have power in Jesus. We have to use it to overcome evil and to enjoy life. With God we don't lose anything, but we gain everything. I hope that one day together we will see the Lamb of God coming in his glory to bring us to the Promised Land. Every person has the right to live well with God forever. My mission was to transmit this message, and I hope with all my heart that people will listen and obey God's voice.

It was a pleasure and an honor for me to be God's writer and to share my testimony with his people. This book was a school for me. I learned a lot through this writing, and I hope that many people will hear God's message and trust him. With thankful heart, I humble myself before the throne of the Lord to thank him for all he has done for me, for you, and for my family in Jesus's name. Amen.

---

249 John 12:36

Biography

I was born in the Eastern of Democratic Republic of Congo, in Africa, in 1965. I earned an associate's degree in management from Institut Superieur de Gestion de Entreprises in Congo. I also earned a bachelor's degree in economic science from the prestigious Universidade Federal do Rio de Janeiro in Brazil. I am conversant in Swahili, French, Portuguese, and English. I have been married for twenty-one years and am the mother of three children. I live in Loganville, Georgia, in the United States.

References

The Holy Bible, New Revised Standard Version, 2005, Cambridge University Press

La Sainte Bible, Version Semeur, 2000, Societe Biblique Internationale.